DETROIT STUDIES IN MUSIC BIBLIOGRAPHY
General Editor
BRUNO NETTL
University of Illinois at Urbana-Champaign

MUSIC AND DANCE RESEARCH
OF
SOUTHWESTERN UNITED STATES INDIANS

Past Trends, Present Activities, and Suggestions for Future Research

BY CHARLOTTE J. FRISBIE

DETROIT STUDIES IN MUSIC BIBLIOGRAPHY / NUMBER 36

INFORMATION COORDINATORS, INC. / 1977 / DETROIT

Cover and title page symbol from a Pueblo rattle, page 42
Book design by Vincent Kibildis
Illustrations by Charlotte J. Frisbie

CONTENTS

PREFACE

T HIS PAPER was originally developed in response to an invitation to participate in the Symposium on the Arts held during the joint meeting of the Southwestern Anthropological Association and the Sociedad Mexicana de Antropologia, March 27-30, 1975 in Santa Fe, New Mexico. Short versions of it were presented both at this conference and at the annual meeting of the Midwest Chapter of the Society for Ethnomusicology, March 1-2 in Milwaukee, Wisconsin.

The author wishes to thank the following colleagues for bibliographic suggestions: Joseph Hickerson, Leanne Hinton, Robert Black, Don Roberts, Marcia Herndon, Joann Kealiinohomoku, Gertrude Kurath, Frank Gillis, George List, Richard Haefer, David McAllester, and Theodore Frisbie. The following individuals deserve thanks for assistance in gathering data for the Appendix: Frank Gillis, Louise Spear, Frank A. Norick, Joseph Hickerson, David McAllester, James B. Wright, Caroline Olin, Bruce Bryan, Holly Chaffee, and Richard Haefer.

The present study, for which the author assumes full responsibility, has benefited from constructive criticisms by the following individuals of an earlier version: Frank Gillis, Bruno Nettl, Don Roberts, Bonnie Wade, David McAllester, Joann Kealiinohomoku, Gertrude Kurath, and Theodore Frisbie. The author wishes to thank these colleagues in particular for their time, suggestions, and encouragement.

Finally, the author wishes to express special thanks to Joyce Giardino and Virginia Bradburry of the Southern Illinois University-Edwardsville Lovejoy Library, for expediting endless interlibrary loan requests, and to Ann Van Horn, Secretary for the Anthropology Department, for her suggestions and careful preparation of the manuscript.

INTRODUCTION

ALTHOUGH SOME SCHOLARS consider the Southwest a well-studied area and urge that efforts be directed elsewhere, the participants in the 1953 Southwestern Conference (American Anthropological Association 1954), Smith (1971), Longacre (1973), Basso (1973), Lange (1975), and many, many others continue to find the research potentials of the Southwest far from exhausted. Present-day southwestern scholars have the advantage of access to tremendous quantities of data from earlier studies of innumerable southwestern topics; thus, we have data on elements of culture which are no longer extant and/or accessible, and information to support numerous studies, especially those which stress processual change and comparisons. While research conditions have not remained static, and in some cases have worsened for nonnative scholars in the Southwest, the potentials for applying and testing contemporary theories and methodologies remain high. That we all share a sense of excitement generated by these potentials, as well as a sense of responsibility for continuing well-established research traditions in order to advance our knowledge and understanding of the Southwest, is surely obvious.

The present paper reflects the belief that periodically it is productive to review critically what we have been doing, and to discuss "where we go from here." As a review paper on Southwestern Indian music and dance research, its purposes are several: to describe the orientations, methodologies, and concerns of past research; to identify present research interests and approaches; and to offer some ideas about research which deserve attention in the future. Data, herein, are presented by decades, after the late 1800s are discussed, and within each decade, music and dance studies are treated separately. The latter division must be understood to be an artificial organizational device, since in many cases in the Southwest, music and dance are inseparable and must be studied together. The paper does not pretend to be definitive;[1] to read, synthesize, and critically evaluate all of the past work relevant to southwestern music and dance would, indeed, take more time and resources than those recently available. Finally, the paper does not claim to reflect a consensus of opinion among my ethno-musicological and dance ethnology colleagues; many of them have not yet had time to react to this paper, and when they do, I am sure discussions will be generated which will be beneficial to us all.

---

[1] No attempt has been made to include *all* information available in archaeological site reports, theses and dissertations, and relevant ethnographies.

THE PAST

ALTHOUGH INTEREST in comparative musicology became established in the nineteenth century especially through the influence of Carl Stumpf, his pupil Erich von Hornbostel, and A. J. Ellis, the first indication of a serious interest in North American Indian music did not appear until 1882, with the publication of *Über die Musik der nordamerikanischen Wilden,* the dissertation of Theodore Baker, an American anthropologist who studied music in Leipzig. The emphasis was not on the Southwest in this work, however, and the century would have ended with little advance in knowledge of southwestern music and dance had it not been for a few anthropologists such as Fewkes and Matthews, musicologists such as Gilman and Fillmore, and several others.

Undoubtedly the most prolific scholar at this time was J. W. Fewkes. With support from Mary Hemenway who sponsored the Hemenway Southwestern Expedition (1887-1894), Fewkes (director of the Expedition after Cushing in 1889) began his years of work among the Hopi and Zuni before the turn of the century. He became the first to use the treadle-run Edison phonograph in the field in 1890, and he recorded[1] numerous songs at Zuni and the Hopi Pueblos, publishing that year on the phonograph's potentials for linguistic and musicological work and Zuni reactions to it (1890a, 1890b). Fewkes incorporated numerous observations on music and dance as well as his own reactions to each in his carefully detailed and illustrated studies of Hopi ceremonialism. Thus, we find publications dealing with summer ceremonials at Zuni and Moqui (1890c), specific dances at Hopi (Lā´-Lā-kōn-ta, 1892 with Owens; Mam-Zraú-ti, 1892

---

[1] See the Appendix for further information on the location of major collections of Southwestern Indian music, as well as suggestions about discographies and other resources.

1880–1899
HOPI SNAKE DANCE KACHINA

11

with Stephen; Walpi Flute Observances, 1894a, Oraibi Flute Altar, 1895a), a provisional list of annual ceremonies at Walpi (1895b), and a description and consideration of purpose and variant forms of Basket Dances in 1899, the year when he joined the Bureau of American Ethnology. Fewkes became interested in the Hopi Snake Dance early in his career, and wrote much about its calendar of events, its meaning, origins, and variable forms in other Pueblos (1891a, 1893, 1894b, 1895c). Fewkes mentioned archaic words in the songs; he found the melodies "wild," "low," "weird," "loud," and "piercing," and he called for team research in order to study the ceremony effectively.

Many of the other writers in the late 1800s focused on the Hopi Pueblos, but it was the Snake Dance alone that received considerable attention. Perhaps predictably, few, except Fewkes, included comments on music or dance movements; instead, the ethnocentric emphasis was on the horrors of holding writhing reptiles in the mouth. Bourke (1884) started the trend, later being joined by Mindeleff (1886), Baxter (1895), Hodge (1896), Rust (1896), and Hough (1899). Baxter's (1895:206) reaction is typical when he refers to one of the snakes as a "wriggling, hissing mass of flesh; . . . the dancer grasps it in his hands and—horrors!—carries the slimy, loathsome reptile to his mouth . . ." Fewkes, and Hodge (1896) were among the few who considered questions of origin, meaning, and distribution of the dance.

Other Pueblo music and dance research included Hough's (1897) comments on the music of the Hopi Flute Ceremony, Thompson's (1889) description of a Pinyon Dance at Jemez, Fillmore's (1896a) study of two Tigua "folk songs," and several works dealing with the Zuni (Klett 1879, Fewkes 1891b, Gilman 1891, Anonymous 1898, and Bourke's 1885 paper on the special Urine Dance held in Cushing's honor which stimulated Bourke's 1888 work on scatology). Some of the ethnographies from this period also include references to songs (cf. Stevenson's 1894 study of Sia).

The music and dance of other Southwestern Indian groups received little attention except for that of the Navajo. After making phonographic records, Washington Matthews produced several important publications on Navajo music (1887, 1889, 1894a, 1894b, 1896, 1897). These considered such topics as song types, specific genres, poetic and archaic elements in song texts, music in ceremonial context, musical instruments, and myth as a mnemonic device; in general, these studies were aimed at disproving Letherman's 1856 statement that Navajo singing was "but a succession of grunts and [was] anything but agreeable" (Matthews 1896).

Matthews also published some of the song and prayer texts in Navajo as well as English. Mindeleff (1898) used interlinear textual translations in his consideration of music used for Navajo Hogan Blessings, and Fillmore (1896b) also studied Navajo songs. An Apache Medicine Dance was briefly described by Russell (1898), but only two or three songs were mentioned.[2]

Many of these early works are typical of the time in their descriptive emphasis and ethnocentrism. Although Fewkes recommended the music of the Hopi Flute Ceremony as "pleasing," many others found, as earlier travelers had, the sounds of the Hopi and other groups to be weird, loud and wild, and full of fierce, bloodcurdling yells, howls, grunts, and whines. Dance movements fared no better; Thompson's (1889:353-354) remarks are typical: ". . . The musicians sawed and thumped . . . . the dancing was monotonous, and consisted only of stamping the ground with the right foot, accompanying the movement by occasionally shaking the gourds." In general, works were not products of specialists; thus, they emphasized scenery, some ethnographic details, and only occasionally mentioned movement and sound. Of course, some of the studies, especially those of Fewkes, Matthews, Stevenson, and Mindeleff, included information useful to specialists today. Fewkes, for example, included data on song types and melodic contours; verbal descriptions of sounds and personal reactions to them; references to borrowed words in texts; and descriptions of costumes, instrumentation, leg-arm-foot and elbow movements, numbers of dancers, relation of body posture to rhythm, and positions and formations of dance groups in plazas. He also provided useful illustrations, suggested a limited use for the term "dance" among Pueblo researchers, and included calendars of both daily and annual events, as well as comments on inter-Pueblo borrowing of dances and change or "decay."

Concern for theoretical issues was minimal. Several considered questions of origin and borrowing of dances and specific songs. Mason's (1897) study of the musical bow includes Pueblo data; the field use of recording equipment, its problems and potentials were evaluated by Fewkes (1890a, 1890b); song structure was of concern to Fillmore (1897) and Matthews (1894b); and Matthews, among others, discussed "meaningless" texts. The few theoretical debates which occurred concerned unilinear evolutionary development schemes in music and attempts to prove them. Benjamin Ives Gilman, a Harvard music professor, was the recipient of

---

[2] Hagemann's (1893) *Great Torture Chant of the Apaches . . .* was not available for review.

many of Fewkes' materials. His analysis of Zuni melodies (1891) included nine transcriptions and a careful description of stylistic and melodic features. Gilman's thesis was that Pueblo music was without a scale and that at "the archaic stage of art" represented by this music, scales were not formed, but forming.

Fillmore, who worked with Alice Fletcher and Franz Boas analyzing tribal melodies, was another professor of music who utilized Matthews' cylinders to provide data for transcription and analysis of Navajo songs (1896b). As a composer, he was interested in using Indian materials in his own compositions and in harmonizing Indian materials for popular use. Theoretically, he was concerned with the evolution of harmonic melody. Fillmore (1896b:240) described Navajo singing as having a "wild animal tone quality, but all this shouting, howling, and whining proceeds along chord lines . . ." He used the results of his analysis to "prove" his theory of latent harmony, saying that Indians have a subconscious sense of harmony, and "Folk-melody, everywhere, the world over, is harmonic melody."

Near the end of the century, the first collection of Indian melodies arranged with harmonies for concert use appeared under the auspices of Carlos Troyer, a musician who had begun field research at Zuni shortly after meeting Cushing in 1888. Thus, at the turn of the century, we have many, valuable ethnographic descriptions (compiled by a limited number of researchers), which contain some data on Southwestern Indian music and dance; numerous popular and ethnocentric statements about both; several attempts to use southwestern data to support unilinear evolutionary theories; and harmonized Indian melodies.

THE FIRST DECADE of the twentieth century saw few changes in the personnel and emphases involved in music and dance research among Southwestern Indians. The Pueblos, especially Hopi, continued to receive most research, and attempts at detailed documentation of entire ceremonies were typical. Voth, a missionary who spent many years at Oraibi, published numerous studies through the Field Museum. Among them were those on Powamu (1901), Oáqol (1903a), and Summer Snake Ceremonies (1903b); with Dorsey, Voth studied the Oraibi Soyal Ceremony (1901) and Mishongnov Ceremonies of the Snake and Antelope Fraternities (1902). These works included daily calendars of events and detailed observations of rituals, with occasional native and English song texts and comments on such topics as song rehearsals, dance motions, repetitions of songs, and archaic and borrowed words in texts. A typical description of dance by Dorsey and Voth (1901:33) follows: "exhausting, rapid, trampling, stepping dance of the Hawk Priest."

Fewkes continued his studies at Hopi (1900, 1901, 1902); Beckwith (1906) attempted a cross-cultural comparison of Moqui and Kwakiutl dance forms, and on the basis of Fewkes' recordings Gilman (1908) published *Hopi Songs,* in many respects a companion volume to his earlier work on Zuni.

Other Pueblos received little attention. Stacey (1907) discussed Zuni ceremonies and melodies and presented five songs he had recorded. Praising the Zuni for their intellectual and dramatic achievements, he found their melodies superior in beauty and originality to those of the Hopi (1907:55). He discussed instruments, fractional intervals, fixed tones, and melodic ranges, based on Troyer's comments about melodic structure, manner of expression, and descriptive characteristics. Stacey's work, however, appears minimal in comparison with Stevenson's (1904) monograph on Zuni ceremonialism, which contains meticulous details on myth, rituals, ceremonies, and dances. Reagan discussed the Corn and Masked Dances at Jemez (1906), describing them with such terms as "crow-hop," "frog leap," "March," "squaws tripping lightly," and the music, as "ear-grating ahooing" (1906:245). Natalie Curtis (1904) provided transcriptions and texts for two Laguna grinding songs, and comments on textual variation, melodic contours, and archaic words in the texts; she also published a melody and text for an Isleta Hunting Song (1906).

HOPI MUDHEAD KACHINA

Matthews continued his research among the Navajo, producing his classic study of the Night Chant in 1902. Apache instruments were briefly mentioned by Hrdlička (1905) and Densmore published one Apache melody (1906). The songs and instruments of the Pima and Papago also received brief mention in ethnographic work by Russell (1908), Brown (1906), Hrdlička (1906), and Kroeber (1909). Harrington (1908) included several song texts in English in his study of Yuma origins, and several southwestern groups were represented in Draper's (1901) general description of southwestern dances.

Historically, the first decade of this century is important because it included the initial work of two women deeply committed to research in American Indian music, Natalie Curtis (Burlin) and Frances Densmore.

Curtis began her work in the Southwest in 1901; although she initially used the phonograph, she soon termed it "unnecessary" and "inadequate," and proceeded to do the rest of her fieldwork armed with notebook, pencil, color box, and camera. Her major work, *The Indians Book,* appeared in 1907 and has since had several editions, including a paperback one (1968). This book is based on "careful and conscientious work" and "trustworthy transcriptions" (Roberts 1927:259); it includes musical transcriptions and native and English texts for 149 songs from eighteen tribes. The emphasis is on the Southwest, especially Hopi and Zuni. The book also contains native illustrations, and while it lacks musical analyses, Curtis did give her ideas about the general characteristics of American Indian music, such as pulsating voice, no harmony, and complex, elaborate, and changing rhythms. She also provided information on cultural contexts for some of the songs and an appendix of interlinear translations.

Frances Densmore, who has rightfully been called "the most prolific collector and publisher of North American Indian Music" (Hickerson 1961:27) also began her work in the 1900s. Starting earlier to study American Indian music with Alice Fletcher, between 1903-1957, she produced over 140 publications on American Indian music, about twenty of which were monographs. Early in 1907 she began phonographic studies and later that year, became associated with the Bureau of American Ethnology, which published all of her monographs as Bulletins, except for the several published by the Southwest Museum.

Another person whose work began in this decade was Edward Curtis. Of the nearly two hundred melodies and associated contextual details he eventually recorded, only a limited number appeared later (with Fillmore's assistance) in his twenty-volume work, *The North American Indian* (1907-1930).

Theoretically no advances were made in the early 1900s. Gilman's *Hopi Songs,* which represented a completion of his inquiry into Pueblo music, emphasized melodic autonomy and lack of scales in Pueblo music. However, the Hopi materials differed from the Zuni ones in that they weakened Gilman's earlier idea that scales might be "forming" at "this archaic stage of art." Gilman's idea that Indian melodies were subject to no restrictions of scale was in direct opposition to Fillmore's work. In addition to his unilinear evolutionary ideas, however, in *Hopi Songs,* Gilman considered some of the methodological problems which remain under discussion in ethnomusicology today. This work includes transcriptions of seventeen songs and a discussion of the difficulties of

transcribing by ear because of cultural-bound expectations about sound.
Using the Ellis cent system for tone measurement, Gilman presented
transcriptions by staff, graph, and contour graph, incorporating additional
symbols for pitch notation on the musical staff versions. He identified
the value of several different opinions on a transcription and suggested
the need for equipment which played recorded sound in reverse and
graphically recorded diaphragm movements. He also discussed the
question of distortion caused by battery-run cylinders. Among other
features, *Hopi Songs* includes a characterization of Pueblo music as music
emphasizing freedom, melody, intervalic division—balance—combination,
thematic development, pitch mutations, downward melodic contours,
and strophic form.

Although Densmore's early work supported the theoretical ideas of
Fillmore, she soon chose to avoid further theoretical considerations, and
turned to an approach which invariably emphasized general ethnographic
details, information on singers, instruments and functions of music,
musical transcriptions, analyses of particular melodic features, and
presentation of results in chart and tabular form.

T HIS DECADE can be characterized by a continued emphasis on
Hopi research and general interest in Pueblo rather than other types
of southwestern music and dance. The studies continued to be those
of anthropologists and general popular writers, and data of interest to
contemporary specialists are somewhat limited. However, horizons did
begin to expand geographically and topically during this time, with
publications on Yuman music, Santo Domingo and Picuris dances, and a
prehistoric flute from Kidder's Pecos excavations. Publication outlets also
expanded slightly; with *National Geographic, Natural History,* and other
magazines, as well as scientific journals including information on Southwestern Indian music and dance, interest was bound to be stimulated.

Hough (1915, 1919) and Voth (1912a, 1912b, 1912c) continued their
work at Hopi, providing details on several ceremonies and Hopi instruments.
Fewkes' (1910) study of the Butterfly Dance, contained within a broader
consideration of the Butterfly in Hopi Myth and Ritual, identified some
similarities between the Hopi dance, songs, and paraphernalia and certain
Rio Grande Pueblo "tablet dances." It also considered the question of
origin linguistically, suggesting that archaic words in the song texts might
be Keres, and it documented amusing clown parodies of Fewkes' use of

the phonograph. Other Hopi work was not of equivalent quality;
Oliver (1911) continued the interest in the Snake Dance with a study
documenting his horrified reaction to the emetic (1911:133, 137) and
perpetuating the usual attitudes by referring to the snakes as "ghastly
burdens" (1911:131). Dance descriptions fared no better; in describing
the steps of the Snake Priests, Oliver says they moved "around the plaza
with a funny, high-stepping motion;" Dellenbaugh's (1915:257) description
of the Somaikoli Dance at Sichumovi states that the "katcina capered
around in frantic spasms of tramps and jumps. . . ."

Zuni music was studied by Troyer (1913) who commented on the deep,
slow, long breathing of Zuni Indians, their belief that sounds have colors
and colors originate from solar vibrations, and their scale of color tones.
The comparative studies of Zuni, Acoma, and Laguna All Soul's Days by
Boas' student, Parsons (1917) and Espinosa (1918), however, made no
reference to music.

Music and dance information from other Pueblos was minimal and
concerned mainly with Tanoan groups. Reagan (1915a, 1915b)
continued his descriptions of corn-masked dances at Jemez and included
a total of thirty-nine melodies from Jemez and three other groups in
his work, *Don Diego* (1914). Twelve Tewa songs were studied by
Spinden (1915a), and two Cañute game songs, one with native text
and translation, were included in Harrington's (1912a) study of this
Tewa game. The Picuris Scalp Dance, replaced by the Fiesta in honor
of San Lorenzo, was briefly described by Pancoast (1918), and Hewett
(1918) described the power and unity of a Keresan Corn Dance and
elaborated on its purpose so that tourists would understand its meaning.
He also commented on offensive, county fair aspects of such dances.

The decade also included collections of San Carlos, White Mountain,
and Mescalero Apache songs by another Boas student, Pliny Goddard,
and a short description of the so-called "Apache Devil Dance" by
Harrington (1912b). Parsons (1919) described the Navajo Squaw
Dance, discussing eligible participants, economics, and dance steps of
girls who single-stepped around their male partners with "fairly lively
hops" while the men shuffled. Spinden (1915b) published a paper
similar to Draper's earlier one in an attempt to describe Southwestern
Indian dances in general terms. Of more interest to specialists is the
paper by Peabody (1917) describing a prehistoric bird bone flute from
Pecos, and raising pertinent questions about sound production techniques
and instrument classification.

THE DECADE of the twenties witnessed several developments in Southwestern Indian music and dance research: an increased number of popular articles on dance, a shift (evidently unplanned) in music studies away from Pueblos toward other areas, some comparative studies, and the appearance of several books on Southwestern Indian dances and several valuable general papers on Southwestern Indian music. More importantly, it was during this decade that the influence of Boas became apparent in Southwestern Indian music and dance research. Although not famous as a theoretician, Boas' emphasis on studying *all* of the arts *in* their cultural context, his rigorous field methods wherein there was an insistence on meticulous recordings of complete details during fieldwork, documentations in the native language, and thorough descriptions of *all* cultural data, and his priority on collecting as much as possible before threats of extinction were actualized, affected all of his students. In the 1920s, information on music and dance increased in amount and detail in the southwestern anthropological literature, and George Herzog, a Boas student, successfully combined German musicology and American anthropology, becoming one of three main contributors to southwestern music research in the process.

The scope of Pueblo dance comments broadened to include many Pueblos besides Hopi, Zuni, and others mentioned earlier. *El Palacio* began publishing articles on specific dances authored by specialists and nonspecialists. Included were Arnold's (1928) comparison of Tesuque and Nambe Hunting Dances (which contained comments on change); an anonymous (1929) article on Green Corn Dances among Eastern Keresans, which included some information on ground plans and changing dance figures; Chapman's (1925) description of the revival and dramatic elements in the Sun Basket Dance at Santa Clara; an anonymous (1928) article on San Ildefonso Animal Dances (which included some descriptions of dance movements), as well as other articles on Hopi, Zuni, and Navajo dances. McIlvaine Parsons (1926) described a performance of the Turtle Dance at San Juan by thirty-seven dancers, and Bailey (1924) provided comments on Taos plays and dances, including a discussion on the necessity of equating the term "dance" with religious ceremonies, as well as comments on changes caused by missionization. E. C. Parsons (1923b) addressed herself to the Fiesta at Santa Ana, in an attempt to correct a lack of adequate information on Saints Days' Dances. This work, which stressed calendars of events, dance personnel, costumes, and kinship affiliations, includes some valuable comments on dance patterns and figures. The same year, another of Boas' students, E. Goldfrank (1923), published a study of two Pueblo feasts, and included song texts, translations of dance songs, and a discussion of the meaning of movements as well as contextual information about dance.

ZUNI SHALAKO KACHINA

Publications on Hopi dance included Parsons' (1923a) work on the Buffalo Dance (which emphasized personnel, paraphernalia, costumes, gestures, and social interaction data), and two studies of the Snake Dance, Oakden-Sturt (1927) and Gianini (1928), of which the latter is more scientific. Work at Zuni was also among Parsons' (1924) activities; her study of winter and summer dance series (1922a, 1922b) emphasized costumes, personnel, paraphernalia, and some schematic group position drawings. Seasonal differences in dance performances were discussed as were the cost of costumes and changes in dance, but specific dance movements and music received little attention. Interest in the Shalako winter solstice ceremony began to develop and continues, today, to remain strong. *El Palacio* carried three articles on Shalako during this decade: the *London Times* reporter Graham's (1923) popular, misinformed comments, Chapman's (1927) calendar of events with references to earlier work by Stevenson, and Chauvenet's (1929) comments which stressed house blessing aspects of the ceremony and "helmet" masks.[3]

Other dance research included studies of Navajo and Yaqui dances. Dances associated with the Navajo Night Chant and Enemyway ceremonial received comments from Guernsey (1920), Parsons (1919, 1921), Kluckhohn (1923), and misinterpretation by Reagan (1929). Kluckhohn (1923) found the quick movements of Yeibichai dancers almost indescribable, while the Bluebird Song was one of his favorites. Guernsey (1920), observing the public Squaw Dance portion of a 1914 Enemyway in Kayenta, found the facial expression of male participants to be "sheepish" and those of their female partners, "bored." Parsons (1921) presented a very interesting paper emphasizing the value of obtaining cross-cultural comments on dance styles as a means of identifying important aspects of style. She included Tewa and Hopi comments on Navajo dancing, which suggest a stereotype wherein Navajo are viewed as "pay[ing] no attention to each other" and not "know[ing] how to step" (1921:24). Bogan's (1925) book on Yaqui Indian dances stressed Holy Week and Pascua ceremonies and contains valuable photographs and interesting data on dance training and differential female-male involvement in dance.

In the area of music, Hopi Kachina songs became available through Fewkes' 1924 recordings released by Gennett Record Company

---

[3] Another work, a study of Pueblo Ritual Dances by Alexander (1927) was not available for review.

$(1925)^4$ and through transcriptions and texts included in the volumes of E. Curtis' study of North American Indians. Even more significant, however, was the fact that the 1920s found two new specialists, Helen Roberts and George Herzog, starting their work on Southwestern Indian music. These two, along with Frances Densmore, dominated the twenties and thirties, gathering much valuable data and doing analytical, distributional, and comparative studies, many of which are still regarded as classics in ethnomusicology today.

Helen Roberts, an anthropologist with a music specialization, has been termed "one of the most active and prolific writers in the field [of North American Indian music]" (Nettl 1956:35). While Roberts has not been particularly concerned with music *in* culture, she has worked on a variety of problems, including history and distribution of styles. Her transcriptions are carefully done and her analyses emphasize structure, rhythm, and melodies. Roberts' earliest work in the Southwest resulted in a comparative study of three Chakwena songs from Zuni and Laguna (1923). The study includes transcriptions, analyses, discussion of some transcription problems, and suggestions about the importance of asking singers, themselves, to verbalize their ideas about form since, as she indicates, they *do* have such ideas! Roberts also teamed up with J. P. Harrington to produce a sizable study of Picuris children's songs (1928) which includes useful comments on variable renditions within the oral tradition.

George Herzog, a student of von Hornbostel, came to America to study anthropology with Franz Boas, and successfully proceeded to weld German musicology and American anthropology. An ethnomusicologist with sound training in linguistics and folklore, Herzog has produced numerous publications on individual and comparative topics, and has contributed greatly to many areas of ethnomusicology, especially those concerned with individual and geographic area styles, and the relation of music to language and other aspects of culture. In 1928 he published an important paper on Yuman musical style; based on fieldwork in 1927, the paper included transcriptions and analyses of thirty-nine songs from the Mohave, Yuma, Mohave-Yavapai, Maricopa, and Southern Diegueño, as well as information on instruments, types and sources of songs, and singing style. Musical analyses emphasized tonality, melody, rhythm, accompaniment,

---

[4] The recordings were made by four singers Fewkes took to the Grand Canyon while he was Chief of the Bureau of American Ethnology. Folkways has reissued the album as FE 4394 (cf. List 1966).

and time, and comparisons with California and Pima Indian music were made. Herzog concluded that Yuman music was unique among American Indian music because of its "rise," its conventionalized hand movements in rattling, and its unusual degree of stylistic integration. The "rise" or shift of melodic weight upward (1928:193) was found in both tonality and formal structure; shifts in melody accompaniment and text were parallel and all combined to yield a well-integrated, consistent form.

Densmore was pursuing Papago fieldwork in 1920-1921 and soon began publishing her results (1921, 1926, 1927a, 1929). The 1921 study contains comparisons with Pawnee materials and the 1929 work was the first of her BAE monographs on Southwestern Indian music. Others were also interested in Papago music during this decade. Stricklin (1923) discussed music, rhythm, and structure; transcription problems; and his own excitement about the potential use of Indian form and rhythmic elements in non-Indian compositions. Davis (1920) examined Harvest Festivals and briefly discussed Papago composition and rehearsal procedures, and Mason (1920) also provided information on selected Papago songs.

Walton (1926) and De Huff (1924) both published bicultural collections; the former's were English, poeticized versions of Blackfoot and Navajo song texts which, according to the author, were not meant to be anthropological contributions. De Huff presented five "authentic" Navajo and Tewa songs. Mention should also be made of the excellent ethnography by Spier, another Boas student, on the Havasupai (1928); this includes valuable information on musical instruments and Havasupai dances.

Among other works on music and dance in the twenties were more general ones. N. Curtis (1921) included transcriptions and native and English texts for two Hopi and one Yuma lullaby in her description of seven American Indian Cradle Songs, and Lehmer (1929) included Navajo and Hopi song texts in his discussion of American Indian music and poetry. Hodge (1920) included information on prehistoric and contemporary Zuni musical instruments in his study of Hawikuh Bonework. The year 1927 was the time of three general publications: a study of Indian music in the nineteenth century (Densmore), and two on Indian music in the Southwest by Jeancon and Helen Roberts. All three papers are valuable resources today; Densmore's contains a useful review of the efforts of Baker, Boas, Fletcher, Fewkes, Gilman and Fillmore, as well as her own (via an editor's footnote). Jeancon's, the least specialized of the three, deals with the close association of music and drama in the Southwest and certain musical features such as phrase length, scale, sequencing, repetition, lack of quarter tones, instruments, functions of music, and the reception of non-Indian music among Southwest Indians. Roberts presents a historic overview which stresses the few systematic studies available by 1927, namely those of Fewkes, Gilman, and Goddard. Her paper includes two musical transcriptions of Goddard's San Carlos material, two songs from Picuris myths, one Tewa love song collected by Harrington, and one Zuni lullaby with native text collected by Parsons. Although Roberts found Apache chant music monotonous and uninteresting, her paper, with its careful transcriptions and concluding echo of Parsons' call for work on southwestern music, "one of the most important and neglected fields for the study of Indian music today" (1927:265), signifies the specialized approaches which were becoming established in southwestern research during the twenties, musically thanks to Herzog and Roberts, and topically, thanks to Boas' influence.

T HE DECADE of the thirties saw continued efforts on the part of Densmore and ethnomusicologists such as Herzog and Roberts to collect and document various aspects of Southwestern Indian music. Several noteworthy comparative studies of musical styles were published, an initial attempt at identifying North American music areas was made, prehistoric instruments were further discussed, and the first publications by natives of the traditions under study appeared. Although Sachs' *World History of Dance* was published in 1937, trained dance ethnologists were not yet available for studies of Southwestern Indian dance, and descriptions continued to be those of both popular writers and ethnographers.

Comments on dance continued to emphasize the Hopi. Although Fewkes died in 1930, the decade brought the publication of Stephen's *Hopi Journal* (1936) and Parsons' tome on *Pueblo Religion* (1939), both of which contain a wealth of information, especially on music and dance in ceremonial context. Other studies of interest include Lawrence (1934), Dutton (1936), and Stephen (1937). Dutton's work compares her observations of a Hopi dance at Jemez in 1932 with accounts of the same event in 1921 by Parsons; the study documents changes in dance, costume, makeup, and musical instruments, as well as the stable elements of this viable dance form. Jones (1932) provided a general description of the Walpi Niman Kachina Dance, with some comments on dance movement, instruments, and meaning, preferring to leave "details" to ethnographers. Colton and Nequatewa's (1933) paper on the Ladder Dance is important in its attempt to use tales to reconstruct features of an extinct dance, and in its joint publication aspect, where one of the authors is a native collaborator (cf. works of Kurath, Hinton, McAllester).

Dances at some other Pueblos—Keresan, Tanoan, and Zuni—were variably described. *El Palacio* carried a paper on Santo Domingo's Green Corn Ceremony (Huebner 1938), two papers by Keech (1934a—Pecos Ceremony at Jemez, and 1934b—Green Corn Ceremony at Zia), a description of the "rare" San Geronimo Fiesta at Taos (Jones 1931b), and a description of Zuni Shalako by Jones (1931a), which movingly conveys the feeling of observers, even though some songs are called "weird incantations" and equated with barking dogs! Keech (1937) also described the "rare" Blue Corn Dance at Santa Clara. Knowledge about Zuni dances was advanced significantly by the study of Zuni ceremonialism done by another Boas student, Ruth Bunzel (1932). Her monograph contains, among other things, voluminous information on Kachina dances and ritual poetry.

KOKOPELLI
HUMPBACKED FLUTE PLAYER

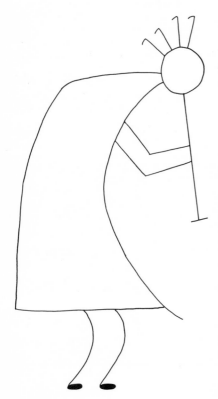

Other Southwestern Indian dance descriptions included Reagan (1934) on Navajo Fire Dances and Montell (1938) on the Yaqui. The latter includes useful photographs and drawings of paraphernalia, descriptions of the Pascola Dance where young dancers step about 340 times a minute and the older ones, even more, details on the Deer, Matachines, and Chapayecas, comparisons with other sources, and a good bibliography.

Music research in the 1930s included specialized studies by trained ethnomusicologists—collectors, comments by ethnographers, and popular articles. Continuing interest in the relevance of archaeology to ethno-musicology was signified, topically, by Boekelman's (1936) study of prehistoric instruments and the discussion of the Humpbacked Flute Player (Hawley 1937 and Parsons 1938), a topic which continues to receive discussion (Miller 1975). The Pueblo so-called "foot drum" was examined by Lowie (1938) and compared with Californian examples.

Research on Pueblo music is represented by Densmore's (1938b) monograph on Santo Domingo Pueblo, Spinden's (1933) study of Tewa song texts collected in 1909-1912, Stephen's (1939-1940) comments on Hopi music and instruments, and King's (1935) thesis on seventy Jemez songs, which Roberts (1972:247) cites as the "only published work of any consequence on Towa Music." Yuman and Yaqui research received attention by Densmore (1932a, 1932b). In a comparative study of Yuman and Pueblo songs (1932a), she contrasted music styles on such

elements as melodic contours and length. Underlying this work was
Densmore's search for "the norm of Indian songs," which she (1932a:
700) concluded was "to be found in their rhythm, not in their melodic
progression." The monograph on Yuman and Yaqui includes musical
transcriptions and analyses for Cocopa, Yuman, Mohave, Yaqui, and
Mayo materials. Densmore also used other southwestern data for
comparative studies and papers on specific aspects of North American
Indian music (1931a, 1931b).

Research on Athabascan music was mainly conducted by anthropologists,
missionaries, and one native during the thirties. Reichard, a Boas student
who had already begun her Navajo work in the twenties, published *Spider
Woman* (1934) and *Dezba* (1939), each of which contains translated,
partial texts and information on music and dance. Franciscan Father
Berard Haile (1938) produced an important paper which considered
Navajo terminological distinctions between chantways, rites, and
ceremonials. Kluckhohn (1933, 1938a, 1938b), Anonymous (1934),
Wyman and Kluckhohn (1938), Woodward (1937), and Walton (1930)
are among others who commented on aspects of Navajo music at this time.
The Wyman and Kluckhohn study is an important one, in its presentation
of *Navajo* classification systems for song ceremonials. Walton's (1930)
work on song patterning, which illustrates strict parallelism, sequencing,
and other organizational principles is also useful. Apache music is
represented by at least one paper by Nicholas (1939), a Mescalero Apache
who collaborated with Opler and Hoijer. Refusing to expose sacred aspects
of the Girl's Puberty Ceremony and giving little information on songs, he
nevertheless provided interesting data on tepee raising songs and the
Mountain Spirit Dance, its costumes, and participants.

George Herzog was extremely busy, collecting and writing in the 1930s
(1930, 1931, 1933, 1934, 1935, 1936a, 1936b). Building on von
Hornbostel's characterization of Indian singing, Herzog (1930) suggested
that North American Indian music contained two basic singing styles,
one with a wide distribution, and one restricted to the Yuman, Pima,
Papago, and their neighbors. He also provided transcriptions and analyses
for the Evans' study of American Indian Dance (1931) and Spier's work
on the Maricopa (1933). Using six Navajo examples collected in the
thirties, Herzog (1934) considered the important question of the influence
of linguistic tones on melodic lines, another topic which continues to
receive attention today. Examples from his numerous field collections
were also used in his 1935 discussion of American Indian song types and
his review-appraisal (1936a) of ethnomusicological efforts in the United

States and comments on methodological guidelines for studying American Indian music in the future. That same year, he published another well-known paper, his comparative study of Pueblo and Pima music styles (1936b). Using thirty-six Pueblo and twenty-one Pima songs recorded in 1927, the work includes native texts and translations, transcriptions and analyses, and a discussion of the distribution of musical traits as well as other details; it remains one of the best comparative ethnomusicological studies in Southwestern Indian music to date.

Another important work which appeared in 1936 was Roberts' music area study. Reviewing the development of interest in southwestern music, which by the thirties had led several individuals to full-time collecting and study, Roberts (1936:5) shows how the Southwest moved from one of the least investigated areas to one of the best in 1936, in terms of actual numbers of recordings made. She then reviews nine popular ideas about American Indian music, plots geographic distributions of instruments, and defines music areas, based on distributions of instruments and vocal characteristics. The work was done in the tradition of Wissler and Kroeber's culture areas. Instruments suggested linking the Southwest and Plains, with the ultimate source being Mexico; this study contains much to recommend it to those interested in Mexican origins. On the basis of vocal music, she linked the Southwest with the Plains and Plateau to form one of six music areas. The linkage was tenuous, as she suggested, because of style mixtures. Identifying Hokan, Shoshonean, Navajo, and Pueblo styles within the area, Roberts urged further work on the multiple components of southwestern music and reminded readers that we "are only on the threshold."

PUEBLO RASP

The work of the thirties mentioned above was also supported by ethnographies of the period. In addition to those mentioned, the works of another Boas student, Bunzel (1932) on Zuni, Forde (1931) on Yuma, Gifford (1931) on Yavapai, Kroeber (1935) on Walapai, White (1935) on Santo Domingo, and Underhill's work on the Papago (1938) are also valuable resources. In the area of music and dance, the extensive collecting activities of Willard Rhodes, George Herzog, and Laura Boulton also deserve mention. Other, more general works worth noting include Fergusson (1931), Buttree (1930), Evans (1931), Fletcher (1934), Densmore (1938a), and Virginia Bailey's (1935) general survey of Indian music in the Southwest.

World War II and its effects resulted predictably in diminished research funds and efforts, and thus, the forties appear scanty by comparison with earlier and later decades. Comments on dance were forthcoming from missionaries, anthropologists, and popular writers. The Hopi Snake Dance generated three more papers (Bogert 1941, Heizer 1944, and Sterling 1941), all of which were concerned with the question of why dancers were never fatally bitten by poisonous snakes. Bogert, an assistant curator of herpetology at the American Museum of Natural History, reported his field study which "proved" all the fangs had been removed, thereby "permanently" settling the question. Hawley's (1948) paper on Los Matachines considered origins, details, and comparative versions of this folk drama. Father Berard Haile (1946a, 1946b) published on the Navajo Fire-Corral Dance and War Dance, stressing meaning and practice as well as calendars of events, and some comments on dance movements. The patterns and ceremonials of the Pueblo, Navajo, and Apache Indians were illustrated and described by Moskowitz and Collier (1949). Papago feasts and the Viikita were respectively studied by Lloyd (1940), and Hayden-Steen (1937) and Jones (1937). The condensed version of the Easter Play among Guadalupe, Arizona Yaqui was described and compared with other versions by Altman (1946-1947).

Musical studies included the Hopi Netquatewa's (1946) brief description of the Hotevilla Flute Ceremony and MacLeish's (1941) publication and analysis of six Hopi songs, collected and transcribed with McAllester's assistance in 1938. Johnson (1940) provided comments on Pima foot drums and their ceremonial context, Herzog (1946) used Pima examples to discuss again sung versus spoken speech, and Nicholson (1945) published four Yuma Los Pastores texts. Athabascan music research included Kluckhohn and Wyman's (1940) study of Navajo Chant practice, a work which includes an update of the Wyman and Kluckhohn 1938 study, and some comments on native categories and what constitutes a good voice; Schevill's (1947) study of types and uses of Navajo songs; Klah's (1942) Creation Myth, complete with texts, and the first in the religion series publications of the Museum of Navajo Ceremonial Art; and Marshall's (1941) general comments on a Navajo drum. McAllester's (1949) doctoral study of Peyote music, although Plains in orientation and data, deserves mention as one of the few outstanding works of the decade, not only for its approach, careful transcriptions and analyses, and identification of characteristic structural features, but also for its comparative data and rich resource material now available to anyone interested in studying Peyote music elsewhere.

APACHE FLUTE

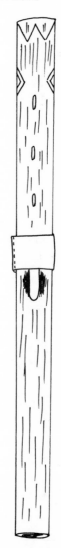

The 1940s also included several ethnographies which contain some helpful data on music and dance; among them are Opler (1941) and Goodwin (1942)– Apache, Spicer (1940)–Yaqui at Pascua, White (1942)–Santa Ana, Whitman (1947)–San Ildefonso, and Joseph, Spicer, and Chesky (1949)–Papago. Also worthy of mention is Sachs' (1940) *History of Musical Instruments,* another outstanding work, and the active collecting activities of J. D. Robb, Odd Halseth, and Archuleta (Roberts 1972:248). Densmore continued her prodigious activity during the forties, producing numerous papers of interest to southwestern specialists (1941, 1943, 1944, 1945, 1947; cf. also Hofmann 1946); and both Boulton (1941) and Chesky (1941) published general descriptions of Southwestern Indian music. Southwestern materials were also among those cited in Van Stone's (1941) comments on Indian songs.

I N ADDITION to the 1953 Southwestern Conference and the resulting special issue of the *American Anthropologist* (1954), the fifties were extremely productive years for ethnomusicologists. The Society for Ethnomusicology was founded in 1955, after the development of a Newsletter in 1953 (which became the Journal, *ETHNOMUSICOLOGY,* in 1958). The first classroom text on non-western music was produced by Nettl (1956); interest in professional training in ethnomusicology expanded rapidly and serious, specialized studies of non-western music became more common. The decade included more work on North American music areas, Lomax's initial work on mapping world musical styles, and the beginning of bibliographic compilations and book and record reviews by ethnomusicologists, all of which showed concern for standards and development of the discipline. Southwestern studies suffered the loss of Gladys Reichard, Frances Densmore, and several others during the decade, but happily for us all, a dancer-anthropologist-ethnomusicologist, by the name of Gertrude Kurath, began to turn her research attentions to the coordinated study of Southwestern Indian music and dance. With her work, specialized studies of Southwestern Indian dance finally began.

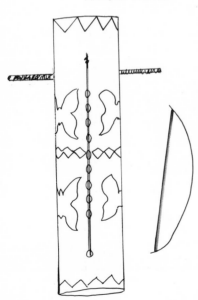

General descriptive articles on various Pueblo dances continued to appear in such publications as *Hobbies, El Palacio, Desert Magazine,* and *Arizona Highways.* Topics included Christmas Eve ceremonies, the Hopi Cow Dance which was brought to Santa Clara, Basket Dance, revival of the Arrow Dance at Nambe, and more on Matachines (cf. Fay 1953; Gallenkamp

1955; Hight 1953; Hurt 1952; Kanellos 1953, 1956; Laski 1957; Lea 1953, 1954; Lewis 1953; McElvary 1951, 1953; Pillsbury 1952; and Roeder 1953). One of the most interesting of these, in its presentation of an individual's feelings about dance participation, is Gallenkamp's (1954) paper on Raphael's last Deer Dance.

The Hopi Snake Dance, or rather its calendar of events and audience reaction to it, was described again by Hall (1953) in a work which used photos taken in 1913 and 1914, one year before the ban on photography was instituted. The origin of Hopi Shalako was discussed by Dockstader (1953), and Cazeneuve (1955) compared a 1954 Zuni Shalako with Stevenson's earlier descriptions. Mead's (1950) work on Ruth Benedict included some of Benedict's comments on Zuni dance, its meanings, calendars, and cultural contexts. Bartoli (1955) wrote an interesting account of the Apache Ghan or Mountain Spirit Dance, which includes some descriptions of dance movement.

Yaqui Easter ceremonies and fiestas continued to receive attention from Barker (1957a, 1957b),[5] Williamson, et al. (1950), Schweitzer and Thomas (1952), and others involved in a University of Arizona team study. Barker's (1958) comparison of functions and culture change aspects of Catholic processions among Yaqui and Keresan Pueblos is particularly noteworthy in its testing of theories suggested by Spicer, Dozier, and Ellis. Equally important is Vogt's (1955) study of the southwestern fiesta system. The latter considers social and economic interaction among seven groups, Indian stereotypes of other Indians and non-Indians, the effect of the Indian Service, and culture change (1919-1952) in dance and other aspects. The emphasis is on the need for data about the *entire cultural situation* rather than just on a procession, a dance, or a group of costumes, and as such, Vogt's comments are well worth remembering.

The decade also included initial papers by Lange on Pueblo dances and Feast Days (1951, 1952a, 1952b, 1953, 1954, 1957). While these contain few ethnomusicological data, they are invaluable resources for dance ethnologists. Although authored by an anthropologist not trained in choreography, Labanotation, or other recording systems, the observations of dance are detailed and documented with care and precision. Lange's emphasis is on dance steps, personnel, and costumes, and many papers

---

[5] There is also some comparative information in Barker's (1957) study of Penitential Processions.

also include information on culture change in dance and rituals, comparisons among other Pueblos, suggestions for future research, and repeated calls for team research in music and dance. Perhaps the most significant of these papers is the 1957 study of the Tablita or Corn Dance (or Green Corn, Harvest, or Feast Dance), which appeared two years before Lange's monograph on Cochiti (1959).

Beginning in the fifties, dance research in the Southwest received a major boost from Gertrude Kurath, who has undoubtedly been the most active researcher in Pueblo music and dance for the past twenty years. Trained as a dancer, choreographer, musician, and art historian, as well as familiar with dance notation systems, Kurath began emphasizing the combination of musicology and dance ethnology in the mid-forties, and in the fifties, turned her own research efforts to the Southwest. This signaled the beginning of scholarly, exact, serious observations by specialists trained to use words and symbols to record dance.

As the decade began, Kurath was busy describing choreology, its methods, and its relation to anthropology in the *American Anthropologist* (1950, 1956a). She also joined those interested in mapping geographic distributions of style in her attempt at establishing choreographic areas of North America (1953). In this study, which ends with a call for preservation of area patterns in recorded form before extinction, Kurath identifies seven areas on the basis of ground plans, typical steps, and body movement patterns. The "complex and all inclusive Southwest" is one such area; it "distinguishes sedentary and nomadic groups with their respective circles and straight lines, yet intermingling; and it shows increasing influence from Mexico in the southerly regions" (1953:71).

APACHE HEADDRESS

Other papers by Kurath used southwestern data in discussing aboriginal American folk dance (1955) and masked clowns (1956b). Nineteen fifty-seven was an extremely productive year; her "Basic Techniques of American Indian Dance" (1957a) and "Notation of a Pueblo Indian Corn Dance" (1957b) included precise comments on posture, foot locomotion, arm movement, and fundamental steps, as well as dance notation scores, discussion of some notation problems, and identification of future research needs. Kurath's regard for native dances as part of viable cultural traditions is clarified in her comments on appropriate use. Her papers on the "Origin of Pueblo Indian Matachines" (1957c) (wherein she reviews much of the earlier work on this topic and supports an Arabic origin for this Christmas choreographic drama), and "Dance Styles of Rio Grande Pueblo Indians" (1957d) also appeared that year. The latter identified five types of dance:

sacred (for hunting and animal increase in winter and for rain and crops in the spring, and both open and closed), strictly native, game animals, secular, and Spanish-derived, as well as the stylistic attributes associated with each. The year 1957 was also the beginning of Kurath's eight years of support from the Wenner Gren Foundation for her monumental study of Tewa Music and Dance (1970).

The following year was equally productive for her. The excellent study of Plaza circuits of Tewa Indian dancers (1958a) contains ground diagrams, circuit prototypes for Tewa dance, comparisons with Keresans, and comments on culture change. "Two Line Dances . . ." (1958b) compares the Deer and Yellow Corn variants. Her paper on Rio Grand Pueblo Game Animal Dances (1958c) is also important. Describing four major types on the basis of cast and choreographic patterns, Kurath presented details on dance movement, meaning, and Plains influence among other data. She also produced a brief description of Cochiti Buffalo Dances (1958d) which includes interesting information on new songs and rehearsals. The following year, another carefully done study, on Cochiti Choreographies and Songs (1959) appeared as part of Lange's monograph on this Keresan Pueblo.

Other resources on Southwestern Indian dance from this decade include Dutton's (1955) careful description of fiestas and ceremonies among Pueblos, Navajos, and Apaches, and Hill's (1954) Bibliography of Pueblo Dances and Ceremonies. Dutton's study, produced as an illustrated handbook, contains useful suggestions to outsiders about appropriate behavior at dances, as well as annual calendars and bibliographies.

Several people were involved in serious studies of Southwestern Indian music during the fifties. Densmore continued her writing, using southwestern data for general papers on numerous topics such as rhythm in the treatment of the sick, words of Indian songs as unwritten literature, and American Indian music (1950, 1953, 1954a, 1954b, 1957a). Rhodes (1956b) and Rexroth (1956) both published important resource materials related to Densmore's career, the year before her death and the publication of her final BAE monograph, Music of Acoma, Isleta, Cochiti, and Zuni (1957b). This last monograph includes data collected in 1928, 1930-1931, and 1939-1940, and is similar in format to her earlier studies.

In addition to his text, Bruno Nettl was active in reviewing the work of others (1953a, 1959), and in furthering ethnomusicological research on numerous problems (1955). His discussion of vocables (1953b) made additional data available on Peyote songs, and his paper on stylistic variety

PUEBLO HEADDRESSES

in North American Indian music (1953c), which resulted from doctoral research, was a prelude to his well-known study of North American Indian musical styles and style areas (1954). Using over ninety percent of the available data, Nettl, in the first attempt since Roberts (1936) to discuss North American Indian music areas, followed the culture area approach, plotting distributions and frequencies of musical style elements rather than instruments or other aspects of music in culture. He described a musical area as "a geographic area whose inhabitants share in a generally homogeneous musical style" (1954:46). Six such areas resulted, and Southwest peoples were grouped as follows: California-Yuman, Athabascan, and Plains-Pueblo. Each area was characterized by specific features; for example, the Plains-Pueblo area included large ranges, terrace types of melodic contours, complex rhythmic organizations, considerable proportion of tetratonic scales, incomplete repetition type of form, and much vocal tension and heavy pulsation (1954:363).

Willard Rhodes was actively editing LPs for the Library of Congress in the fifties and writing on North American Indian music (1952a, 1952b, 1956a). His extensive annotated bibliographic survey (1952b) is extremely useful, especially in its discussion of the relationship between music research and anthropology and its identification of problems needing future research. It remains one of the few such works (cf. Hickerson [1961] for a later one).

David McAllester began actively publishing on Athabascan music in the fifties. After preparing text translations and notes, which include a good description of mnemonics, for the Navajo Creation Chant album issued by Peabody Museum (1952), he published his well-known study of Navajo Enemyway Music (1954). The first half of this work emphasizes the public part of this Navajo ceremony which is held to remove bad effects of foreign ghosts. Transcriptions, native and English texts, and analyses of secular songs are included. The second part is devoted to discussion of social and aesthetic values as reflected in Navajo music and culture. *Enemyway Music* represents a pioneer effort at studying values cross-culturally and it continues to be an outstanding contribution. Other studies by McAllester included a functionalist approach to music in White Mountain Apache Culture (1956a), which discusses categories of songs and a "functional aesthetic," i.e., one where music is appreciated if you know what it is for, and commentaries on the Navajo Great Star and Coyote Chants (1956b). Another work, a study of the technological construction and use of an Apache fiddle (1956c), continues to be one of the few sources on this instrument.

Other ethnomusicological activities were also related to southwestern studies. Krader (1956) prepared an up-to-date bibliography of Herzog, and McAllester (1955), as well as others, were active in publishing reviews of southwestern records. Haywood's (1951) bibliography of North American Folklore and Folksong is a useful reference for some southwestern groups, and Robb's (1952-1953) description of his own folk music collection publicized this resource. Then too, Alan Lomax (1959) called for a "new science of musical ethnography" which would relate world musical styles to the total human situation embracing music. His ideas and collaboration with Victor Grauer soon led to the development of cantometrics (Lomax 1962), a method for mapping world song styles and relating performance style to social and communication systems within culture. This approach was later expanded to include choreometrics, the study of dance as a measure of culture (Lomax 1968).

Anthropologically, resource works by Dockstader (1957) and Seder (1952) became available in the fifties, as did numerous ethnographies and papers containing useful information on certain aspects of music and its relation to culture. Among the latter were Reichard's *Navaho Religion* (1950), Astrov's (1950) work on the Navajo concept of motion, Smithson's (1959) *Havasupai Women,* DiPeso's (1956) study of the Pima, Becker's (1954) summary of Papago music on the basis of Densmore's work, and further information about prehistoric instruments (Kidder 1951, Miles 1953, and Morris 1959). Voegelin and Euler's (1957) "Introduction to Hopi Chants" is another important work from the fifties; designed to correct the lack of attention given to secular chants, the authors used content and discourse analysis in their study which includes information on temporal occurrence, personal chanting styles, and other topics. They offered four suggestions for future research: comparison of village chanting styles; acculturation in chanting; linguistic differences between spoken, chanted, and sung Hopi; and Rio Grande influences on Hopi chanting. To date, further work has come only from Black (1964, 1966, 1967).

T HE SIXTIES saw an expansion in the numbers and activities of specialists in Southwestern Indian music and dance research. Theoretically, the emphases continued to be on functional approaches, although some comparative and distributional studies continued, and some researchers began utilizing the eliciting procedures of ethnoscience or cognitive anthropology. Geographically, in dance the emphasis was on the Tewa and Tiwa Pueblos; scholars, in addition to Gertrude Kurath, included Don Brown, Don Roberts, Arnold Pilling, and Native Americans, including Antonio and Carlos Garcia, Juanito and Gregorita Trujillo, and Bobby and Joe Lujan.

A landmark contribution to the anthropological world is represented in Kurath's "Panorama of Dance Ethnology," which appeared as a review essay in *Current Anthropology* (1960a). The work surveys the development of dance ethnology, discusses its scope, delineates problems shared with anthropology and other disciplines, and describes basic choreographic procedures and practical considerations.

Kurath also produced several general papers (1960b, 1961-1962) and several detailed studies of Tewa Dance (1963, 1965). "Calling the Rain Gods" (1960b) discussed gesture levels in Rio Grande Keresan Dance and her paper on "American Indian Dance in Ritual and Life" (1961-1962) identifies the Southwest as one of five major choreographic areas. Kurath's study of Tewa Choreographic Music (1965) discusses six basic choreographic types: rain cloud, yellow corn, tablita, deer, game animal, and social; two basic steps: the common ántege (foot lifting) and péci (deer step or double bounce used in tablita and game animal dances), as well as the pervading Pueblo device of rhythmic shifts, halting beat (ta'a')—pause, and other structural features. The proceedings from a symposium she organized on dance ethnology include many thought-provoking papers on dance education, ethnology, and the public (cf. Brown 1963).

Of equal value are the papers by some of her native American collaborators; the Garcias' (1968) study of "Ritual Preludes to Tewa Dances" contains excellent information on song and dance composition and transmission processes. "Tanoan Invocation Gestures" (A. Garcia and J. and G. Trujillo 1966) documents a demonstration given by the authors at the 1965 Society for Ethnomusicology meetings in Albuquerque.

Don Brown, who wrote a senior honors thesis on Taos Dance for Harvard in 1959, focused his attention on native classification systems in Taos Dance (1960), and the influences of culture contact and acculturation on historical development of Taos Dance (1961). The latter elicited a reply from Pilling (1962), questioning the beginning dates of Taos dances for tourists and other issues. Other Taos information can be found in Anonymous (1967), the Lujans' (1962) paper on the origin of the Hoop Dance, and Sloan's (1962) reply.

PUEBLO DRUM

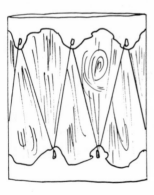

The Hopi Snake Dance generated another book, by Forrest (1961), which incorporated Fewkes' and Voth's earlier observations and excellent old photographs (dating 1906-1908). Joann Kealiinohomoku (1967) also began publishing results of her research on Hopi dance, offering, among other things, an interesting comparison of Hopi and Polynesian gestures, use of space, interaction with other dancers and audiences, and costumes. Zuni Shalako was described again (Gonzales 1966) and the Zuni Kumanche was discussed by Raymond (1960-1961).

Tress (1968) offered a comparison of Japanese and Yaqui deer dances[6] and several authors added to the literature on Matachines (Robb 1961, Feder 1962, Lea 1963-1964, Hurt 1966). Goodman (1968) studied the form and function of the San Juan Basket Dance and Robb (1964) discussed rhythmic patterns in Santo Domingo Corn Dances and the problems of working where the use of recording equipment is forbidden. The decade also included three highly useful publications on Pueblo Dance. Roberts' (1964) brief guide presents seven basic, etic categories for Rio Grande Pueblo Dance (sacred, semi-sacred, corn, animal, borrowed, social-round, and jazz-popular), and describes each in a very readable style. Roediger's (1961) and Brown's (1962) studies of Pueblo ceremonial costumes contain much culture change and comparative information as well as excellent illustrations. The Meads (1969) also briefly described Southwestern Indian dance.[7]

Ethnomusicological activities were numerous and diverse in the sixties. The decade included the publication of two landmark volumes, Merriam's (1964a) *Anthropology of Music,* and Lomax's (1968) *Folk Song Style and Culture.* Both of these works have already had far-reaching effects on ethnomusicologists, anthropologists, and dance ethnologists, and familiarization with them as well as the professional reactions to them (cf. Merriam 1966, Nettl 1970, Driver 1970, Downey 1970, McLeod 1974) is recommended to anyone thinking of specializing in the study of arts in culture.

In southwestern studies, the number of ethnomusicologists interested in Southwestern Indian music increased during the sixties, and research expanded geographically as well as topically. The continuing anthropological interest

---

[6] For other Yaqui information, see Kurath (1966a) and Wilder (1963). The latter incorporates Spicer's 1940 fieldnotes and represents a careful study of culture change in the Deer Dance, especially changes reflected in songs, dance, and associated meanings.

[7] Navajo dances were given a cursory description by Michener (1966a, 1966b). More useful, but equally brief information occurs in Snyder's (1966) review of the film, "Navajo Night Dances."

in prehistoric instruments, reflected in Bakkegard (1960), Bakkegard and Morris (1961), and Frisbie (1967a) culminated in the first attempt at synthesis by Brown (1967). In a prize winning paper on the distribution of prehistoric musical instruments in the Southwest, Brown, through library and museum studies, plotted the distribution of idiophones and aerophones, suggesting two basic strata for instruments—one prior to 1000 A.D. (divided into pre- and post-600 A.D.) and the other, post 1000 A.D. (divided into pre- and post-1300, when wide variety becomes the norm). The topic today remains in need of further research, especially in view of the tremendous amount of archaeological information available, and the ever-changing knowledge of Mexican-Southwestern ties.

List (1962, 1964, 1968), Harvey (1966), and Black (1964, 1966, 1967) focused research efforts on Hopi music. Black's work on ritualized chant language developed aspects of ideas presented earlier by Voegelin and Euler (1957), investigating freedom, restriction, style, and social inter-action dynamics of grievance and rabbit hunt chants. List's (1968) work on the Hopi as composer and poet is important in its documentation of song types, text themes, borrowed language, interaction between composer and performing group, and the dynamic process of individual and group composition of public Kachina dance songs. His other papers (1962, 1964) discuss changing functions of songs, "meaningless syllables," and additional topics.

Research in Navajo music and culture was actively represented by McAllester (1961, 1968, 1969), McAllester and Brown (1962), and McAllester's student, Johnson (1964), who became Frisbie in 1965 and continued publishing (1967b, 1968). Among topics studied by McAllester were comparisons of Navajo, Apache, and Pueblo music, and Navajo and Apache song structure and content, and vocal style. Frisbie studied Navajo Corn Grinding Songs and the relation between myth, ceremony, music, and prayer in Kinaaldá or the Girl's Puberty Ceremony; she also wrote a general paper on the Navajo House Blessing Ceremony, the topic of her dissertation research. Anthropological works on the Navajo affecting understanding of aspects of music in its cultural context included Aberle (1967) who was answered by Opler (1968 and 1969), Anonymous (1965), Clark (1966), Lamphere (1969), Link (1960), and Wyman (1962, 1965).

Information on Taos music was included in a brief description of a Taos Peyote Ceremony (Collins 1968) and more detailed discussions of Round Dance and other song forms by Roberts (1965) and Brown (1968). The latter two works, record reviews, also illustrate, as do Kurath (1966b) and Ortiz (1969b), the expectations ethnomusicologists have of record companies which are producing albums of Southwestern Indian music.

Using southwestern data, ethnomusicologists also addressed themselves to other questions, both theoretical and nontheoretical, during the sixties. Kurath considered use, rhythmic patterns, and comparisons in her study of the Yaqui Pascola sena'asom rattle (1960c). She also questioned the validity of Nettl's Plains-Pueblo music area grouping in her comparative study of Plains and Pueblo songs (1969), calling for a "rethinking" of the music area concept and an approach which considers numerous songs, dance behavior, functions, and environmental factors. Nettl, who produced more ethnomusicology texts (1960, 1964, 1965), considered the question of polyphony in North American Indian music (1961), and in an excellent paper (1966), discussed the very important question of just how western civilization has influenced North American Indian music. This work describes musical style changes; impoverishment of text, repertory, style, and dances; expansions of contacts; new religious movements; and the development of Pan-Indianism. Acculturation in North American Indian music also continued to receive attention from Rhodes (1963), who used songs with English words or total English texts and social dances as indicators of culture change.

Nettl returned to a consideration of music areas in 1969, revising his own earlier six-part scheme, which was based on materials then available and the notion that *a* music or tribal repertory is homogeneous. In 1969, he suggested establishing a two-part scheme—"areas which have the traditionally required degree of homogeneity and of trait clustering" and those which do not (1969:184-185). In the former group would be those areas with one or two predominant types of structural song or composition and reasonably homogeneous singing styles. Using this approach, Nettl suggested five areas: East-Plains-part of the Plateau-Eastern Great Basin-Pueblo-and Eastern Apache; Eskimo; Northwest Coast and Coastal Salish; Western Basin and Northern California; and California-Yuman and Navajo. These can be otherwise viewed as two, large, heterogeneous areas (Eskimo-Northwest and Eastern Plains-Pueblo . . . .) and two smaller, more homogeneous ones, Western Basin and Yuman-California-Navajo. Avoiding definitive conclusions, Nettl encouraged flexibility in the use of the music area concept and asked for continued discussion of this classificatory tool.

Diversity in ethnomusicological interests, so characteristic of the sixties and the present, is reflected in other publications which used, if not emphasized, Southwestern Indian musical data. Summaries on Southwestern Indian music were produced by McAllester and Brown (1962) and Boulton (1968), and Black (1965) reviewed ethnomusicological studies in the American Southwest. Interests in ethnohistory, currently increasing in so many disciplines, began to become apparent in ethnomusicology with Crawford's (1967) study of Jesuit and other documents pertaining to American Indian music. List (1963) continued considerations of the relationship between speech and song. Rhodes (1967) compiled a bibliography for Helen Roberts, and his own professional activities and collections were described by Korson and Hickerson (1969). Gillis and Merriam (1966) produced a bibliography of theses and dissertations in ethnomusicology and folk music, and Hickerson (1961) also produced an invaluable resource, his "Annotated Bibliography of North American Indian Music . . . ," the updating and publication of which would be of great assistance to many scholars.

THE PRESENT

1970–1976

THE PRECEDING REVIEW HAS, above all else, suggested that serious studies of Southwestern Indian music and dance by specialists in ethnomusicology and dance ethnology have only been in existence for several decades, although the literature is voluminous. The emphasis has shifted from straight description to careful recording on tape, film, in notebooks, and in Labanotation or other script, of details of music and dance, and to ethnographic inquiries aimed at clarifying unending cultural context questions. Functional and comparative studies have increased and distributional studies, revised in view of accumulating data, and interests in specialized problems of acculturation, ethnohistory, and prehistory, as well as in testing theoretical developments in linguistics and structural and cognitive anthropology are becoming apparent.

Dance research among Southwestern Indians in the 1970s has already produced several landmarks. Kurath's *Music and Dance of the Tewa Pueblos* (1970) remains unique in its combination of music and dance research and will be a model well worth emulating in the future. Working with four dimensional patterns which document music, dance movement, words, and ground plans, she investigated types of dance, dance calendars, intertribal borrowing, and cultural change in Tewa music and dance, as well as numerous other topics, such as the Puebloization of the Eurasian Matachines. Don Roberts' (1970) study of origins, development, and structure of Tewa Round Dances and the Garcias' (1970) study of Ritual Preludes and Postludes are also included in the Kurath volume, which needs only to be accompanied by Ortiz' (1969a) *Tewa World* to result in an unusually well-rounded picture (cf. McAllester 1972). Other contributions to the study of Pueblo Dance include Sweet's (1976) approach to Tewa Dance which is based on Ortiz' ideas, and La Vigna's (1976) work on the process of composition in San Juan Turtle Dances.

PUEBLO BULLROARER

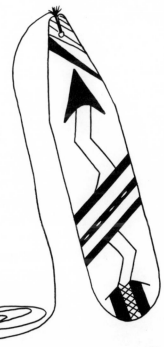

The Dance Ethnography Data Inventory (Risner 1973) represents another useful resource. Designed to develop and use methods for discovering and cataloging extant dance data in anthropological literature, the inventory presents, in etic categories, data on dance from six cultures in the Human Relations Area File, including the Havasupai.

Another outstanding resource is the CORD *Research Annual,* volume 6 (1974), which includes the proceedings of the 1972 CORD conference on "New Dimensions in Dance Research: Anthropology and Dance—The American Indian." Among the papers is one by Brown (1974) discussing the reconstruction of dance in the prehistoric Southwest on the basis of archaeology and ethnographic inference. Yaqui Easter ceremonies are discussed by Spicer (1974) and Painter (1974; cf. also Litvinoff 1973). Spicer's work is particularly valuable in its comments on history and cultural context, and distortion of the Deer Dance into a romantic Mexican Dance by the Ballet Folklorico. Litvinoff's earlier paper is likewise worthwhile in its discussion of movement patterns and theatrical elements. Hieb (1974) and Snyder (1974) discuss symbolic aspects of dance, and Lomax, Bartenieff, and Paulay (1974) provide further discussion of their choreometrics project. The volume also includes clearly stated field methodology suggestions by Kealiinohomoku (1974a) and discussion of some physiological aspects of dance (Taylor 1974). This latter topic has recently received different treatment by Reyman (1974), who hypothesized that Pueblo dance patterns are conditioned by natural rhythms found in both participants and their environments.

Other papers in this CORD volume, including Kealiinohomoku (1974b), Merriam (1974), and Valenzuela (1974), do much to indicate where some anthropologists and dance ethnologists believe dance research should go from here. Kealiinohomoku (1974c), who is currently synthesizing other aspects of her research on the role of dance in Hopi society (see Kealiinohomoku 1970b), calls for study of *dance culture*—namely, the who, what, when, why, where, and hows—, an approach which delineates the choices, the involvement of all participants (including non-dancers), and takes account of the heterogeneity of dance and culture. Merriam, as he has done earlier (1964a, 1964b), emphasizes a holistic approach which incorporates viewpoints and concerns of social scientists and those in the humanities. He outlines three major responsibilities and calls for an anthropological study of dance which views it as human behavior and concept, as well as product or body movement. Valenzuela (1974) raises other issues, especially ethical ones including problems of adapting native dances to nonnative productions (also of concern to Spicer, Kurath,

and others), the need for honest collaboration with native peoples,
and banning performances in artificial, nonnative settings. These
approaches are among those Valenzuela believes will enable dance
ethnologists to aid in the regeneration rather than the degeneration
of native rituals and dances.[8]

Ethnomusicologists have also been active. In addition to major textbooks
(Hood 1971, McAllester 1971c) and work in music education (Ballard
1970, 1973, and the special issue of *Music Educators Journal,* October
1972), a special bibliography of Kurath has been prepared (Kealiinohomoku
and Gillis 1970); a directory to United States and Canadian sound collections,
compiled (Briegleb 1971); a selected bibliography on American Indian music,
published (Heth 1974); the impact of western music on Native American
music, considered (Nettl 1975); and Ethnomusicology has appeared for the
first time in the *Annual Review of Anthropology* (McLeod 1974). There
has also been much ethnomusicological research on specific problems in the
Southwest thus far in the seventies. Continued interest in ethnohistorical
documents is reflected in Stevenson (1973a, 1973b), whose papers contain
a reassessment of Baker's earlier work and much information on the Southwest from sixteenth-eighteenth century documents. Brown (1971) has
discussed problems of reconstructing prehistoric musical sounds and styles,
and Roberts (1972) has provided a useful review paper on ethnomusicology
of Eastern Pueblos. Other Pueblo studies have included Weinman (1970),
Gordon (1972), R. Rhodes (1973), and B. Tedlock (1973).

Athabascan research thus far has included Frisbie's (1970) study of the
Navajo House Blessing Ceremony, Chiao's (1971) consideration of process
and change in the transmission of Navajo ceremonial traditions (a work
which includes suggestions for training future singers which are particularly
interesting in view of recent NIMH support for such training), Frisbie's
(n. d.) work on the ethnography of Navajo ceremonial performance,
and Frisbie and McAllester's (n. d.) life history of a Navajo Blessingway
singer. Additional studies include Wyman's (1970) publication of three
Blessingway myths and one Mountainway myth (Wyman 1975) collected
earlier by Father Berard Haile, Carrither's (1971) study of the Enemyway
Squaw Dance, McAllester's (1970) discussion of Blessingway songs,
further comments on Navajo and Apache styles (1971a, 1971b), analysis
of a Shootingway Snake Song (n. d.) and his study of Navajo music,

---

[8] Among works which consider the implications of Pueblo dance for other dance
forms are those by Kealiinohomoku (1970a) and Litvinoff (1974).

co-authored with one of his native collaborators, Douglas Mitchell (n. d.). The latter paper reveals one native's classification of Navajo music and also discusses hymns, Peyote music, rock and country and western music, and other forms under "new music." Among other relevant Navajo studies are Harrison's (1973) consideration of women in Navajo myth, Gill's (1974) analysis of prayer acts, Wagner's (1975a, 1975b) considerations of Peyote ritual, and Witherspoon's (1975:56-64) discussion of Enemyway symbolism in his volume on Navajo kinship and marriage. Apache music in an Iroquois setting has been treated by Kolinski (1972) who provides interesting comparative data on variation through time and transmission.

Ware (1970)[9] has discussed culture change in Pima music, calling for studies which consider nontraditional arts and their performers, and those which include consideration of adaptations western musical forms and instruments make to non-western settings. The new ethnographic study of *Pima Shamanism,* co-authored by anthropologist Bahr, shaman Gregorio, interpreter Lopez, and editor Alvarez (1974), contains much information on a shaman's role as well as song texts. Ritual oratory of the Pima and Papago has received further attention from Bahr (1975). Contemporary information on the acculturative dance music, Waila, of the Papago has been provided by Griffith (1976). Havasupai music received brief attention from Reilly (1970), and the text of a medicine song along with comments on composition, structure, and other aspects, have been published by Hinton and Hanna (1971), one of Hinton's Havasupai collaborators. Among on-going ethnomusicological research today are Leanne Hinton's (1974) linguistic analysis of Havasupai songs, Ginger Farrer's study of the Mescalero Apache Girl's Puberty Ceremony (Herndon 1974 and Farrer 1976), Richard Haefer's (1975) study of Papago conceptions of the domain of music, Frisbie's study of the transmission of Navajo ceremonial medicine bundles, and McAllester's analysis of contemporary Native American music.

Other works of interest to ethnomusicologists and dance ethnologists include the 1972 republication of Moskowitz and Collier's 1949 study of Southwestern Ceremonial Dances, Bahti's (1970) *Southwestern Indian*

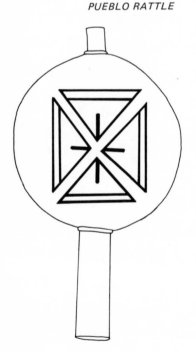

PUEBLO RATTLE

---

[9] This study was based on fieldwork done during the Indiana University Summer Linguistic Institute Program, directed by Carl Voegelin. Among other ethnomusicologists who have participated in the program are Gerald Johnson, who worked among the Mohave in 1965 and Stephen Wild, who studied Tewa music at the Hopi First Mesa in 1966 (Kealiinohomoku 1975).

Ceremonials, Hofmann's (1970) brief description of American Indian musical instruments, Collaer's (1973) *Music of the Americas,* Kurath's (1974) summary of American Indian music and dance, and Dutton's (1975) *Indians of the American Southwest.* Then too, Rothenberg's (1972) inclusion of southwestern song texts and Dennis Tedlock's (1972) presentation of formal Zuni narrative tales and stories of "The Beginning" in works which are striving to develop procedures for "total translations" of native poetry (or translations which account for kinesic and paralinguistic aspects of oral performance), are also worthy of study by anyone who has ever tackled the problem of textual translations.

THE FUTURE

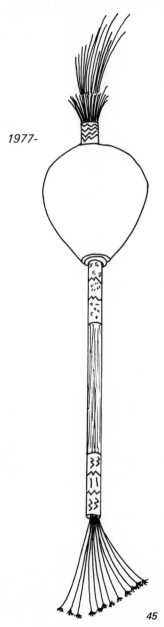

Q UESTIONS ABOUT where we should go from here and what needs to be done are likely to be answered on the basis of personal evaluations of where we have been, specialized interests in particular problems, and biases toward or against relevant theoretical developments in the allied disciplines of anthropology, ethnomusicology, and dance ethnology. These questions are not new in Southwestern Indian music and dance research; Parsons (1939), Lange (1951), Rhodes (1952b), Kurath (1960), Black (1965), Roberts (1972), and Risner (1973) are among those who have commented upon them in the past. Reviews make it obvious that uneven attention has been given geographic regions, musical and dance styles of particular peoples, questions of culture change, the arts in their cultural context, comparative studies, and the like, and I am sure none of us feels at a loss to identify things that need to be done.[1]

One of the options is to answer such questions topically; this approach, for me, as well as for others in some previous instances, would include, among other things, the extension of integrated studies of music and dance to Keresans and other southwestern groups, comparisons of Keresans and Tanoans, and intervillage and regional studies, all in an attempt to achieve a definition of Pueblo, Navajo, Havasupai, and other southwestern peoples' dance and music. It would also include

---

[1] An identification of productive future research emphases will be among the topics of concern during a seminar planned for 1978. In April of that year, the School of American Research in Santa Fe, New Mexico, will host an Advanced Seminar on Southwestern Indian Ritual Drama. The emphasis will be on ceremonial music and dance, and participants will include: Robert Black, Don Brown, Ginger Farrer, Charlotte Frisbie, Richard Haefer, Leanne Hinton, Joann Kealiinohomoku, David McAllester, Don Roberts, and Barbara Tedlock.

1977-   continued work on the process of composition; identification of mnemonic devices; specific studies of individual song and dance genres; comparisons of Navajo and Apache puberty ceremonies; identification of Pueblo influences on Navajo music and dance and vice versa; a comprehensive study of North American Indian musical instruments which synthesized prehistoric, ethnographic present, and contemporary data; a restudy of older materials utilizing new equipment and new theoretical and multidisciplinary approaches; continued preparation of bibliographic resource materials; and detailed studies of change in all music and dance forms in the Southwest, which would relate ethnographic information to contemporary influences and responses to change.

Another option, however, and the one I prefer, is to answer questions of "where we go from here" by identifying trends and general developments which appear worthy of further research effort. Among my own priorities is an increased emphasis on *the human beings* involved in music and dance. While in some cases our etic information is now excellent on the *products*—the song structures, singing styles, dance movements, and costumes, we continue, for much of the Southwest, to know little about the *people* involved in the music and dance arts. Such research would emphasize questions such as who are the dancers, singers, composers, and other participants in music-dance events? How are they selected, by whom, and by what criteria? How do they learn and teach others, and what part of these processes is reflected in enculturation experiences of those who do not become dancers and musicians? What are the components of the creative process? How do the people compose, sing, play instruments, and dance? What models, mnemonic devices, formulas, and patterns do they follow and how much freedom exists for individual artists? How do they interact with each other and with audiences, both native and foreign, and what kind of feedback effect results? How do their roles as artists relate to other aspects of their lives?

Simultaneous with the above, we need to broaden our studies and do a better job of delineating music and dance *in* culture. This entails many of the same kinds of questions, but an expansion of them past the individual sound, instrument, performance, and the body paint. What else is actually going on during a public Kachina dance? Who is interacting with whom during the Yeibichai part of the Navajo Night Chant, with what kind of behavior, for what purpose, and in what roles, and how do all of these things reflect other cultural patterns and preferences?

We also need to make a concerted effort toward eliciting native
classification systems and native viewpoints, and all of the implied,
related value judgments. What is "music," what is "dance" to a
Havasupai? What kinds of taxonomic categories do native peoples
have, what kinds of linguistic descriptions for the process of singing,
dancing, composing, and using instruments? What stereotypes exist?
What are the native performance standards? What is "good" or "bad"?
Are artists compared, discussed, and evaluated overtly or covertly,
and if so, what constitutes good-bad, success-failure, or other distinctions
that may be recognized by native peoples? How do these relate to other
values in culture, and how do these organizing principles differ from
the evaluations and categories which have been imposed by nonnative,
scientifically trained researchers and observers?

Persistence and change in music and dance is also badly in need of research
effort. Studies which identify sources of and influences causing change;
which document directions of change, examining native reasons for
acceptance, fusion, rejection, or other reactions to contact; which
document the process of borrowing and the differential rates within
the context of cultural history are much needed. More attention needs
to be given to nontraditional forms, the show dances, the new musics,
the tribal country and western groups and rock bands, the effect of
television, radio, films, and records on native musics, and yes, even the
effect of the availability of cassette and other recorders which enable
native peoples to record their own musics. Native Americans' views of
change need delineation as do their preferences as these are expressed
in record purchases of native or nonnative musics, and attendance-
participation patterns at traditional and nontraditional music and dance
events. Likewise, these studies need to be extended beyond musical
style and dance forms to the humans, their changing preferences and
roles. And, even if a number of specialists perfer to work on integrated
documentation of traditional styles, attention must be given to the *mutual*
effect of contact, borrowing, and attending powwows and ceremonials.

Another issue to which we must all give attention, both as individual
scholars and as members of our respective disciplines is the question of
ethics. With increased self-consciousness and group identity more than
obvious among contemporary American Indians and other peoples today,
we need to consider very carefully and discuss openly what we are doing
and why. Among the endless issues worthy of serious thought are: the
propriety of publishing and otherwise using music and dance materials
(especially ceremonial ones) out of their cultural contexts; proper

recognition and collaborators through joint publications and proper credits and financial reimbursements; expansion of opportunities for training in our specialized disciplines so that interested native peoples become, in fact, equipped to do their *own* research; and assistance and support of native efforts to preserve traditions. These are only a few of the issues which have recently surfaced in our disciplines and each of them demands and must receive our prompt, serious attention.

In addition to increasing our recognition of responsibilities to our native collaborators, we also need to expand our efforts at disseminating our research results to the public. To do so involves decisions about avenues of dissemination; development of standards for records, tapes, television programs, instrument displays and the like; and development of scientifically credible materials suitable for classroom use at all levels of education, which convey music and dance in their cultural contexts, rather than frozen sound and static dance poses.

We should also continue several of the recent trends, namely those which emphasize ethnohistorical research, investigations and reconstructions of prehistoric music and dance though ethnographic inference and analogy, and increased interaction with archaeologists—be they questioning the real purpose of the so-called "ball-courts" of the Hohokam or pondering the latest research work on Mesoamerican-Southwestern ties. Similarly, we should become or remain aware of current developments in linguistics. It is true that topics such as the interrelationship of all levels of speech-song-dance movement, procedures for text translations, and "meaningless syllables" all need further work, but it is also true that the broader developments of transformational linguistics have implications for what we are doing. As Basso (1973:245) wonders, could not some of Kurath's choreographic data be restated in the form of ordered transformational rules which, when accompanied by explicitly stated contextual restrictions, could be used to generate acceptable dance-step sequences?

Implied in all of the above is, of course, another development, which, given the rapid expansion of both ethnomusicology and dance ethnology, simply must happen and happen soon—namely, team research. There are few Kuraths around, and most of us consider ourselves fortunate if we can successfully combine music and anthropology or dance and anthropology. However, just as the days are gone of unquestioned acceptance of nonnative researchers, their recorders, cameras, notebooks, and wallets full of grant money, so, too, has passed the time when we can proceed without merging our individual skills. Gone are the years

when we could make excuses for not dealing with the cultural context
aspects of the musics and dances we study, when we could use the
infancy of our disciplines to explain piecemeal views of particular song
styles, musical genres, or body movements. We have treated music,
dance, and culture as separate entities for too long, and the time has
come to utilize multidisciplinary team approaches to research, so as to
have end products which are unified. Only then will our research reflect
the arts *in* culture instead of our own preferences, specialized training,
and the historical isolationism typical of our disciplines in earlier days.

As we continue our research on Southwestern Indian music and dance,
then, let us recognize that *our* studies, too, reflect the "fractured
paradigm" Basso (1973:247) has found typical of southwestern ethnology
and contemporary American anthropology in general. Let us not regret
that the days of vague descriptions and a handful of dedicated collectors
are over, and that our disciplines have passed the hurdles of infancy,
and have moved into a time when there are many specialists, orientations,
and approaches. Let us continue with our eclectic or singular theoretical
preferences and our diverse activities, for there is room for us all, but
let us remember that without working together, none of us, be we
ethnomusicologists, dance ethnologists, linguists, archaeologists, or
ethnologists, will ever achieve an understanding of the arts *in* culture.

APPENDIX

For serious students of Southwestern Indian music and dance, knowledge
of available discographies, phonorecordings and phonofilm archives is
crucial. The task of compiling data on these resources, however, represents
another full-length project which is, at present, far from complete. Thus,
the suggestions given below are not to be considered exhaustive or definitive.

M ANY USEFUL BIBLIOGRAPHIES and bibliographic aids have already
been cited in this paper; see, for example: Densmore, 1927b;
Dockstader 1957; Gillis and Merriam 1966; Haywood 1951; Heth 1973;
Hickerson 1961; Hill 1954; Kealiinohomoku and Gillis 1970; Korson
and Hickerson 1969; Krader 1956; Kurath (with Garcia) 1970; Nettl
1955; Rexroth 1956; Rhodes 1952b, 1956b, 1967; Robb 1952-1953;
D. Roberts 1972; H. Roberts 1927; and Stevenson 1973a, 1973b. In
addition to these, the following resources should also be consulted: The
"Current Bibliography and Discography" section and the Book, Record,
and Film Review sections of the journal, *ETHNOMUSICOLOGY;* similar
bibliographic and review sections in *The American Indian Quarterly, The
Dance Research Journal* (formerly *CORD News*), and *Media Anthropologist;*
the "Available Resources" and "New Publications and Releases" sections
in the Society for Ethnomusicology's bimonthly *S.E.M. Newsletter;*
and current scholarly publications dealing with Southwestern Indians.

DISCOGRAPHIES

PHONORECORDING COMPANIES

A MONG THE RECORDING COMPANIES which market both traditional and contemporary Southwestern Indian music for both native American and other audiences are: Indian House, Canyon Records, and Thunderbird, Sound Chief, and Tom Tom Records. Folkways, Caedmon, World Pacific, Request, and Candalario Records, and the Library of Congress and the Taylor Museum are among others who have also issued such albums.

ARCHIVES

T HE MAJOR RESOURCE to consult in this area is the *Directory of Ethnomusicological Sound Recording Collections in the United States and Canada* (Briegleb 1971). In the spring of 1975, the author sent inquiries to eight of the archives and museums listed in this directory, in an effort to begin the task of documenting the location and accessibility of major sound recordings of Southwestern Indian music. All responded but only four did so in detail; these included the Archive of Traditional Music, Indiana University (through Frank Gillis, Associate Director); the Archive of Folk Song, Library of Congress (through Joseph Hickerson, Archive Head); the Southwest Museum (through Bruce Bryan, Curator); and the Lowie Museum of Anthropology at the University of California at Berkeley (through Frank Norick, Principal Museum Anthropologist).

An ongoing project which will develop a computerized index to collections at the Arizona State Museum in Tucson (Holly Chaffee, Curator), and the current taping of cylinder holdings of the Museum of Navajo Ceremonial Art in Santa Fe (Caroline Olin, respondent) by the Smithsonian prevented both of these archives from responding at this time. Cataloging projects at both the Archive of Southwestern Music at the Fine Arts Library, University of New Mexico, Albuquerque (James B. Wright, Director) and the Archive of World Music at Wesleyan University, Middletown, Connecticut (David McAllester, respondent) have also to date made detailed responses impossible. Among the Archive of Southwestern Music holdings are donations by J. Dear Robb, Odd Halseth, Charlotte J. Frisbie, and Don L. Roberts. The Archive of World Music includes over one hundred and fifty hours of tapes; among the Southwestern Indians represented are the Navajo, Zuni, Apache, Acoma, and Havasupai, and among the donors are David P. McAllester, Odd Halseth, Charlotte J. Frisbie, and Leanne Hinton. Many of the collections of ceremonial music in this archive are accessible only by special arrangement.

The information received concerning collections of Southwestern Indian music at Indiana University, University of California at Berkeley, Library of Congress and Southwestern Museum follows.

ARCHIVES OF TRADITIONAL MUSIC, INDIANA UNIVERSITY
057 Maxwell Hall
Bloomington, Indiana 47401
Prepared by Frank Gillis and Louise Spear

In general, all collections represent original recordings. The accession number is the archive key reference number. The number of hours of recorded time for each collection is approximate. Collections given with Options 2 and 3 are restricted; copies for off-campus use cannot be made without permission from collector. Copies can be made of collections marked Option 1 or where collector is deceased.

Tribe/Collector	Date	Accession No.	Option	Hours	Description
ACOMA					
Leslie White	1927-1928	60-004-F	1	.5	various dance songs
Joel Maring	1961	62-015-F	1	1.5	various dance songs, translations of texts
ACOMITA					
George Herzog, Leslie White	1927	Pre 54-101-F	3	1	festival, ceremonial, kachina, deer hunting, buffalo dance, Comanche dance, Mescalero Apache dance, Navajo dance, American songs
APACHE					
Pliny Goddard	1909-1910, 1914	Pre 54-103-F	2	5	ceremonial flute, Gotal, puberty, deer, war dance, Gan songs, prayer
Morris Opler, et al.	1931	Pre 54-014-F	3	7.5	unidentified material
Joseph Dixon	1908-1909?	Pre 54-102-F	2	10 min.	hunting, dance songs
Danquole Variakojis	1959	59-31-F	3	17.5	female puberty ceremony, devil dance songs, rain songs, prayers, war dance songs, deer ceremony, morning prayer songs, social dance songs, lightening songs, love songs

Tribe/Collector	Date	Accession No.	Option	Hours	Description
Danquole Variakojis	1960-1961	63-035-F	3	19.5	dance, snake, drinking, lightning, girls', horse, life, medicine, love, etc., songs
Bruno Nettl	1952	Pre 54-015-F	3	2	peyote, sun dance, hand game, Scout, love songs
COCHITI					
George Herzog	1927	Pre 54-106-F	3	1	various dance songs, (including corn, buffalo, hunting), spring ceremony songs
HOPI					
Natalie Curtis (Burlin)	ca.1902	Pre 54-027-F	2	2.5	kachina, buffalo, snake, rabbit hunt, antelope, lullaby, war, Powamu songs, narrations
Natalie Curtis (Burlin)	1903	Pre 54-118-F	2	3	various kachina and other dance songs, grinding songs, lullabies, etc.
G. Herzog, Kennard	1939	Pre 54-234-F	3	1.5	kachina dance, buffalo dance, gambling, children's songs
Robert Black	1957-1959	60-005-F	3	7.5	large variety of dance songs (e.g., butterfly, kachina, fertility, hunting, buffalo), various other songs (e.g., gambling, lullaby, game, children's)
Joann Kealiinohomoku	1965	67-056-F	3	5	interviews on music and dance, kachina dance, Inter-Tribal Indian ceremonial
George List	1960	68-233-F	3	8.5	basket dances, lullabies, children's songs, chants, kachina dance songs, social dance (butterfly, buffalo) songs, Tewa water snake ceremony, corn grinding songs, interviews concerning music

Tribe/Collector	Date	Accession No.	Option	Hours	Description
ISLETA					
Robert J. Smith	1964	67-161-F	3	3	tales, story songs, grinding, dance, love, guilt songs, large amount of interview material on life history
JEMEZ					
Odd S. Halseth	1949-1950	61-018-F 61-024-F 61-039-F	2	1.5	buffalo, love, women's, harvest, hunting, ceremonial, corn grinding, dance songs
LAGUNA					
George Herzog	1927	Pre 54-122-F	3	1	corn grinding, medicine, rain dance, Comanche dance, kachina dance songs
MARICOPA					
Naomi Ware	1965	66-20-F	3	7	ant song cycle, dance songs, morning songs, interviews on musical terms, basketry terms, kinship
Naomi Ware	1966	67-109-F	2	5	round dance, origin myth, bluefly songs, interviews
MOHAVE					
George Herzog	1927	Pre 54-124-F	3	2	dance, other songs
Gerald Johnson	1965	66-031-F	3	15	dance music, interviews about dances
NAVAJO					
Gladys Reichard	ca.1930	Pre 54-039-F	1	13	much unidentified material, some song, some speech; some identified as prayer, rain and harvest songs, death and life (speech), deities (speeches)

Tribe/Collector	Date	Accession No.	Option	Hours	Description
Washington Matthews	ca.1912-1913	Pre 54-125-F	2	3	much unidentified material, girls' puberty dance, planting, grinding songs
George Herzog	1933	Pre 54-301-F	3	4.5	game, yeibichai, ṅdá, rain ceremony, corn grinding, horse songs
PAPAGO					
Ruth Underhill	1942	Pre 54-042-F	3	3.5	ceremonial songs and speeches for war, salt pilgrimage, curing, Wikita ceremony, agriculture, girl's puberty rite
SAN JUAN					
George Herzog	1927	Pre 54-134-F	3	1.5	various dance songs, love, children's, war, dawn, corn songs
TAOS					
George Herzog	1927	Pre 54-138-F	3	1.5	ceremonial-social songs, dance, women's, race, boys', love songs
Helen H. Roberts	ca.1935	Pre 54-209-F	3	2	various dance songs
ZUNI					
George Herzog	1927	Pre 54-144-F	3	1	social, kachina and other dance, corn grinding songs
Robert Black	1957-1959	60-005-F	3	1	social dance, clown, butterfly dance, rain dance, kachina dance, rabbit hunt chant, mudhead songs

The following is to be considered a "very rough and not necessarily complete listing" of the vast holdings of the Southwestern Indian music in the Library of Congress. The italicized word *Includes* indicates that the collection includes whichever Southwestern Indian group is specified plus some materials that are not Southwestern, if no further specifications are given.

Abbreviations

Cas.	Cassette
Cyl.	Cylinder
D.	Disc
Rec.	Record
Rl.	Reel
T.	Tape
n.d.	no date

Tribe/Collector	Date	AFS No.	Description
ACOMA			
Robert Black	1957-1966	14,059-14,077	19-10" Rl. *Includes* Acoma and other Pueblo materials
APACHE (unspecified)			
Russell Mosby	n.d.	13,554-13,573	20-10" D. *Includes* Apache
Willard Rhodes	1951-1952	14,618-14,625	8-10" Rl. *Includes* Apache
J. D. Robb	n.d.	15,459-15,523	65 T. (63-7", 2-5"). *Includes* Apache
GENERAL SOUTHWEST			
John S. Candelairo	last 20 years	16,982-16,983	2 Cas. Western American Indian Tribes
Frances Densmore	1933	6,182-6,195	14-12" Rec. *Includes* Southwestern Indians
Frances Densmore	n.d.	10,515-10,744	230-16" Rec. *Includes* Southwestern Indians
William N. Fenton	n.d.	10,879	1-7" Rl. Southwestern Indians
William Rhodes	n.d.	10,090-10,094	5-10" Rl. *Includes* Southwestern Indians

Tribe/Collector	Date	AFS No.	Description
Willard Rhodes	1941-1943, 1947, 1949	12,097-12,295	55-10" D; 144-12" D. *Includes* Southwestern Indians
J. D. Robb	n.d.	9,610-9,628	19-12" Rec. *Includes* Southwestern Indians
J. D. Robb	1950s	12,332-12,342	9-7", 1-5" and 1-3" R1. Folk and Indian music of the Southwest
Margaret Valiant	1939	3,314-3,334	20-12" Rec. Southwestern Indians

HOPI

Tribe/Collector	Date	AFS No.	Description
Robert Black	1957-1966	14,059-14,077	19-10" R1. *Includes* Hopi and other Pueblo materials
Laura Boulton	1933	16,152-16,277	126 D. *Includes* Hopi and other Southwestern groups
J. Walter Fewkes	n.d.	11,321-11,325	5-10" D. Hopi
J. Walter Fewkes	n.d.	11,783-11,792	10-12" D. Hopi
J. Walter Fewkes	n.d.	14,046-14,051	6-10" test pressings, Hopi (identification not certain according to catalog card)
J. Walter Fewkes, Washington Matthews, Roland Dixon, Benjamin Gilman, Herbert Spinden	1891-1910	4,214-4,477	264 Cyl. *Includes* Hopi
Willard Rhodes	1951-1952	14,618-14,625	8-10" R1. *Includes* Hopi
Various Collectors	n.d.	11,077-11,299	167-12", 79-10", 40-8", 7-7" D. *Includes* Hopi and other Southwestern materials
Various Collectors	n.d.	15,403-15,423	21-10" T. *Includes* Hopi materials dubbed from Victor 20043
Not available	1903	4,043-4,052	10 Cyl. Hopi
Not available	n.d.	8,900-8,911	12-16" Rec. *Includes* Hopi

ISLETA

Tribe/Collector	Date	AFS No.	Description
Alan Lomax	n.d.	6,317-6,327	11-16" Rec. Isleta
Various Collectors	n.d.	11,077-11,299	167-12", 79-10", 40-8", 7-7" D. *Includes* Isleta and other Southwestern materials

Tribe/Collector	Date	AFS No.	Description
JEMEZ			
Laura Boulton	1933	16,152-16,277	126 D. *Includes* Jemez and other Southwestern groups
LAGUNA			
Robert Black	1957-1966	14,059-14,077	19-10" R1. *Includes* Laguna and other Pueblo materials
B. A. Botkin, Arthur Semmig, John P. Harrington	1944	7,611	1-16" Rec. *Includes* Laguna songs
MESCALERO APACHE			
Laura Boulton	1933	16,152-16,277	126 D. *Includes* Mescalero Apache and other Southwestern groups
Not available	n.d.	13,502-13,503	2-12" D. *Includes* Mescalero Apache and other Southwestern materials
NAVAJO			
Laura Boulton	1933	16,152-16,277	126 D. *Includes* Navajo and other Southwestern groups
Frances Densmore	n.d.	6,895-6,896	2-10" Rec. *Includes* Navajo
J. Walter Fewkes, Washington Matthews, Roland Dixon, Benjamin Gilman, Herbert Spinden	1891-1910	4,214-4,477	264 Cyl. *Includes* Navajo
David P. McAllester	1957	12,081-12,086	6-7" R1. Navajo
David P. McAllester	1958	12,321-12,331	11-7" R1. Navajo
Geoffrey O'Hara	1914	14,078	1-10" Rl. Navajo
Willard Rhodes	1951-1952	14,618-14,625	8-10" Rl. *Includes* Navajo
J. D. Robb	n.d.	15,459-15,523	65 T. (63-7", 2-5"). *Includes* Navajo
Omer C. Stewart	1938	15,090-15,097	8 D. *Includes* Navajo
Various Collectors	n.d.	11,077-11,299	167-12", 79-10", 40-8", 7-7" D. *Includes* Navajo and other Southwestern materials
Mary C. Wheelwright, Anna Barrington	1920s	14,773-14,778	6-10"Rl. *Includes* Navajo and other Southwestern materials
Not available	n.d.	751-819	69 Rec. *Includes* Navajo and other Southwestern materials

Tribe/Collector	Date	AFS No.	Description
Not available	n.d.	13,502-13,503	2-10" D. *Includes* Navajo and other Southwestern materials
Not available	1937	14,058	1-12" D. Navajo

PIMA

Tribe/Collector	Date	AFS No.	Description
Various Collectors	n.d.	11,077-11,299	167-12", 79-10", 40-8", 7-7" D. *Includes* Pima and other Southwestern materials

PUEBLO (unspecified)

Tribe/Collector	Date	AFS No.	Description
Willard Rhodes	1951-1952	14,618-14,625	8-10" Rl. *Includes* Pueblo
J. D. Robb	n.d.	15,459-15,523	65 T. (63-7", 2-5"). *Includes* Pueblo
Various Collectors	n.d.	11,077-11,299	167-12", 79-10", 40-8", 7-7" D. *Includes* Pueblo and other Southwestern materials
Mary C. Wheelwright, Anna Barrington	1920s	14,773-14,778	6-10" Rl. *Includes* Pueblo and other Southwestern materials
Not available	n.d.	751-819	69 Rec. *Includes* Pueblo and other Southwestern materials

SANTO DOMINGO

Tribe/Collector	Date	AFS No.	Description
Frances Densmore	n.d.	3,976-4,000	24 Cyl. Santo Domingo Pueblo
Frances Densmore	n.d.	14,315	1-10" Rl. *Includes* Santo Domingo

TAOS

Tribe/Collector	Date	AFS No.	Description
Russell Mosby	n.d.	13,554-13,573	20-10" D. *Includes* Taos

ZUNI

Tribe/Collector	Date	AFS No.	Description
Robert Black	1957-1966	14,059-14,077	19-10" Rl. *Includes* Zuni and other Pueblo materials
Leland A. Coon	n.d.	8,362-8,473	112-12" Rec. *Includes* Zuni
J. Walter Fewkes, Washington Matthews, Roland Dixon, Benjamin Gilman, Herbert Spinden	1891-1910	4,214-4,477	264 Cyl. *Includes* Zuni

LOWIE MUSEUM OF ANTHROPOLOGY
Kroeber Hall, University of California at Berkeley
Berkeley, California 94720
Prepared by Frank Norick

The present list does not contain information on hours and is to be considered "rough". The museum is currently transcribing old cylinders and tapes onto modern master tapes and upon completion of this work, catalog records will be updated for easy reference.

Tribe/Collector	Date	Accession No.	Description
HAVASUPAI			
Leanne Hinton	August 1964	24-309	11 Mohave Bird songs; 2 solo songs; 40-45 Supai Circle Dance songs
		24-310	30 Supai (identification not certain according to catalog record) Sweathouse songs; 4 Navajo Sweathouse songs; 1 narrative song about mountain sheep; 6 Navajo Horse songs; 4 Circle Dance songs; 10 miscellaneous songs of Supai, Chimshueve and Mohave
		24-311	7 Rock and Roll; 6 Circle Dance songs; 13 miscellaneous songs of Supai, Yavapai, Apache, Mohave, Navajo and Paiute; 16 Sweathouse songs; 3 songs associated with stories and 7 miscellaneous songs
		24-312	2 Navajo Horse songs; 7 Sweathouse songs; 11-13 Sweathouse songs; some shaman songs; 2 narrative songs and some Supai tales in English
Elman Service	not available	24-326	12" 78 rpm record; songs, Havasupai; label: Indian songs w/sound-script reporters, etc.

Tribe/Collector	Date	Accession No.	Description
HOPI			
D. N. Lehmer	May 1925	14-2365	grinding song
		14-2372	spring song
		14-2373	Mudhead song
		14-2374	buffalo song
		14-2375	buffalo song
		14-2376	acting song
		14-2379	lullaby
		14-2380	gambling song
		14-2381	harvest song
		14-2382	bathing song
		14-2388	betrothal song
		14-2389	spring song
		14-2391	game of little folks
		14-2392	clown song
		14-2393	clown song
J. Walter Fewkes	unknown	24-6	Powamu kachina-bean harvest song; Mucaiasti kachina-buffalo hunt song
		24-7	Soyohim kachina song; Makwatu-rabbit hunt song
		24-8	Pawik kachina-duck ceremony song; Malo kachina song
		24-9	Tacab kachina song; Humis kachina song
MARICOPA			
Leslie Spier	1929-1930	24-327	10" 78 rpm record; copy of 14-2699/700
		14-2699	Mt. Killdeer song; hiding game song
		14-2700	rat song; Long Tumanpa song
		24-328	10" 78 rpm record; copy of 14-2701/2
		14-2701	buzzard song
		14-2702	Ivaoo song and Ilyacac song
		24-329	10" 78 rpm record; copy of 14-2703/4
		14-2703	Ivaoo song; buzzard song
		14-2704	Long Tumanpa song; Mt. Killdeer song
		24-330	10" 78 rpm record; copy of 14-2705
		14-2705	rat song; hiding game song

Tribe/Collector	Date	Accession No.	Description
NAVAJO			
Derrick N. Lehmer	1925-1928	14-2366	Apache Dance song
		14-2367	Apache Dance song
		14-2368	Apache Dance song
		14-2369	"Ntah" Summer Dance song; Squaw dance
		14-2370	Navajo Summer Dance song
		14-2371	Yeibichai Dance song
		14-2377	Navajo Summer Dance song
		14-2378	Navajo Summer Dance song
		14-2383	Yeibichai song
		14-2384	Navajo Summer Dance song (identified as the Pig Song by the Hopis and considered humorous)
		14-2385	Navajo Summer Dance song
		14-2386	bluebird song
		14-2387	Navajo Summer Dance song (for rain)
		14-2390	Navajo song (for sewing moccasins)
		14-2540	2 gambling songs—beaver and mountain lion; 1 comic song
		14-2541	2 Navajo War songs
		14-2542	1 Navajo Medicine Chant song and 1 Navajo War Dance song
		14-2543	2 Navajo Love songs composed by singer
PAPAGO			
P. J. A. Schinhan	1932-1933	24-27	Doctor Dance songs 1 and 2; Test recording of Mr. Spark of Radio Dept., University of California
		24-28	2 Medicine Man's songs
		24-29	1 "Wuakah" and 1 Wine song
		24-30	Cactus song and Ghost Dance song
		24-31	Song of the Bat and Song of the Bats
		24-32	Kukuhes-Song at the return of the Warriors; Meli-tcu'tah-Morning song of the Wuakah
		24-33	2 Magic songs of the Coyote
		24-34	2 Medicine Man's songs

Tribe/Collector	Date	Accession No.	Description
		24-35	1 Adolescence song and 1 Morning song of the Wuakah
		24-36	2 Medicine Man's songs
		24-42	Medicine Man's songs 3 and 4
		24-43	Medicine Man's songs 5 and 6
		24-44	Medicine Man's song 7
C. DuBois and Waterman	1909	24-247	Tape from cylinder including Papago music
Waterman and Goddard	early 1900s	24-248	Tape from cylinder including Papago music
J. A. Mason	1919	24-273	Tape from cylinder including Papago music
J. A. Mason and J. D. Dolores	1919	24-274	Tape from cylinder including Papago music
J. D. Dolores	1919	24-275	Tape from cylinder including Papago music
		24-276	Tape from cylinder including Papago music
		24-277	Tape from cylinder including Papago music
		24-278	Tape from cylinder including Papago music
SANTA CLARA			
D. N. Lehmer	December 15, 1926	14-2544	Family song of the Pueblo Indian: Get up sleepy head; Navajo Hunting song
		14-2545	Eagle Dance song
		14-2546	1 Pueblo Indian Drinking song (peyote); 1 song–The Deserted Lover
		14-2547	Love song: The Deserted Lover
		14-2548	1 Pueblo song: The Good Old Times; 1 Victory song over Navajos

Note: Excerpts from category 14 tapes of the **HOPI**, **NAVAJO**, **PAPAGO**, and **PUEBLO** tribes can be found in Accession Nos. 24-284, 24-285, 24-291, and 24-292.

SOUTHWEST MUSEUM
Highland Park
Los Angeles, California 90042
Prepared by Bruce Bryan

The Southwest Museum holdings of Southwestern Indian music include twenty-four wax cylinders of Santo Domingo Pueblo music collected by Frances Densmore (Library of Congress AFS No. 3,976-4,000) and one 10'' reel which includes music from Santo Domingo Pueblo as well as from other non-southwestern Indians. The latter was also recorded by Frances Densmore (Library of Congress AFS No. 14,315).

REFERENCES CITED

Aberle, D.

1967   "The Navaho Singer's 'Fee': Payment or Prestation?" In *Studies in Southwestern Ethnolinguistics*, edited by D. Hymes and W. Bittle, pp. 15-32. The Hague: Mouton and Company.

Alexander, H. B.

1927   *The Ritual Dances of the Pueblo Indians.* Denver, Colorado.

Altman, G. J.

1946-1947   "Yaqui Easter Play of Guadalupe, Arizona." *Masterkey* 20:181-189; 21:19-23, 67-72.

American Anthropological Association

1954   *American Anthropologist*, edited by E. W. Haury, vol. 56/no. 4, pt. 1 (Southwest Issue).

Anonymous

1898   "Music of the Zuni Indians of New Mexico." *Musical Courier* 37:1.

1928   "The Animal Dance at San Ildefonso." *El Palacio* 24:119-122.

1929   "The Green Corn Ceremony." *El Palacio* 27:48-50.

1934   "Navaho Goat Song." *Masterkey* 8:188.

continued **Anonymous**

 1965 "Internal Revenue Service Rules Navaho Sings' Medical Expense."
      Indian Voices, April, pp. 5-6.

 1967 "Our Lady of Guadalupe Day in Taos." *El Palacio* 74:4, 34.

Arnold, C.

 1928 "The Dance at Nambe." *El Palacio* 24:26-28.

Astrov, M.

 1950 "The Concept of Motion as the Psychological Leitmotif of Navaho Life
      and Literature." *Journal of American Folklore* 63/no. 247:45-56.

Bahr, D.

 1975 *Pima and Papago Ritual Oratory, A Study of Three Texts.* San Francisco:
      Indian Historian Press.

Bahr, D., J. Gregorio, D. Lopez, & A. Alvarez

 1974 *Piman Shamanism and Staying Sickness.* Tucson: University of
      Arizona Press.

Bahti, T.

 1970 *Southwestern Indian Ceremonials.* Las Vegas, Nevada: K. C. Publications.

Bailey, F. M.

 1924 "Some Plays and Dances of the Taos Indians." *Natural History* 24:85-95.

Bailey, V.

 1938 "Indian Music of the Southwest." *El Palacio* 44:1-3.

Baker, T.

 1882 *Über die Musik der Nordamerikanischen Wilden.* Leipzig: Breitkopf
      und Härtel.

Bakkegard, B. M.

1960 "Music in Arizona Before 1912." *Journal of Research in Music Education* 8/no. 2:67-74.

Bakkegard, B. M., & E. A. Morris

1961 "Seventh Century Flutes from Arizona." *Ethnomusicology* 5/no. 3:184-186.

Ballard, L.

1970 *The American Indian Sings.* Bk. 1. Santa Fe: Ballard Music Company.

1973 American Indian Music for Your Classroom. Four LP-Cassette package with teacher's guide and additional materials. Phoenix: Canyon Records.

Barker, G. C.

1957a "The Yaqui Easter Ceremony at Hermosillo." *Western Folklore* 16:256-262.

1957b "Some Aspects of Penitential Processions in Spain and the American Southwest." *Journal of American Folklore* 70:137-142.

1958 "Some Functions of Catholic Processions in Pueblo and Yaqui Culture Change." *American Anthropologist* 60:449-455.

Bartoli, J. F.

1955 "The Apache 'Devil Dance.'" *Musical Courier* 152/no. 8:8-10.

Basso, K.

1973 "Southwestern Ethnology: A Critical Review." In *Annual Review of Anthropology*, edited by B. Siegel, no. 2, pp. 221-252. Palo Alto, California: Annual Reviews, Inc.

Baxter, R. H.

1895 "The Moqui Snake Dance." *American Antiquarian* (and *Oriental Journal*) 17:205-207.

Becker, D. M.

1954 "Music of the Papago." *Smoke Signals* 6/no. 5:2-4.

Beckwith, M. W.

1906 "Dance Forms of the Moqui and Kwakiutl Indians." *Proceedings of International Congress of Americanists* 15/no. 2:79-114.

Benedict, R.

1959 "They Dance for Rain in Zuni." In *An Anthropologist at Work,* by M. Mead, pp. 222-225. Boston: Houghton-Mifflin Company.

Black, R. A.

1964 *A Content-Analysis of Eighty-One Hopi Indian Chants.* Unpublished Ph.D. dissertation, Indiana University.

1965 *Ethnomusicology Research in the American Southwest.* Paper presented at Annual Meeting of Society for Ethnomusicology. Albuquerque, New Mexico

1966 "Hopi Rabbit-Hunt Chants: A Ritualized Language." In *Essays on the Verbal and Visual Arts,* edited by J. Helm. *American Ethnological Society Proceedings,* pp. 7-11.

1967 "Hopi Grievance Chants: A Mechanism of Social Control." In *Studies in Southwestern Ethnolinguistics,* edited by D. H. Hymes and W. Bittle, pp. 33-53. The Hague: Mouton and Company.

Boekelman, H. J.

1936 "Shell Trumpet from Arizona." *American Antiquity* 2:27-31.

Bogan, P. M.

1925 *Yaqui Indian Dances.* Tucson, Arizona.

Bogert, C. M.

1941 "The Hopi Snake Dance." *Natural History* 47:276-283.

Boulton, L.

1941 "Recent Recordings in Southwestern Music." *Teacher's National Association Proceedings (1940),* ser. 35, pp. 128-131.

1968   "La musique rituelle des Indiens de l'Amerique du Sud-Ouest." In
          Encyclopedie des musiques sacrees, edited by J. Porte, vol. 1, pp. 117-125.
          Paris: Labergerie.

Bourke, J. G.

1884   *The Snake-Dance of the Moquis of Arizona.* New York: Charles
          Scribner's Sons.

1885   "The Urine Dance of the Zunis." *Proceedings of American Association
          for Advancement of Science* 34:400-404.

1888   Compilation of notes and memoranda bearing upon the use of human
          ordure and human urine in rites of a religious or semi-religious character
          among various nations. Washington, D. C.

1895   "The Snake Ceremonials at Walpi." *American Anthropologist* 8:192-196.

Briegleb, A., comp.

1971   Directory of Ethnomusicological Sound Recording Collections in the
          United States and Canada. *Society for Ethnomusicology,* Special Series,
          no. 2. Middletown: Wesleyan University Press.

Brown, D. N.

1959   *The Dance of Taos Pueblo.* Unpublished Senior Honors thesis,
          Harvard University.

1960   "Taos Dance Classification." *El Palacio* 67/no. 6:203-209.

1961   "The Development of Taos Dance." *Ethnomusicology* 5/no. 1:33-41.

1962   *Masks, Mantas, and Moccasins: Dance Costumes of the Pueblo Indians.*
          Colorado Springs: Taylor Museum.

1963   "Museums and Dance Ethnology." In *Dance Ethnology, Dance Education
          and the Public*—a symposium organized by G. P. Kurath. *Ethnomusicology*
          7/no. 3:239-243.

1967   "Distribution of Sound Instruments in the Prehistoric Southwestern
          United States." *Ethnomusicology* 11/no. 1:71-90.

1968   "Review of Two Indian House Records: Round Dance Songs of Taos
          Pueblo." *Ethnomusicology* 12/no. 2:304-305.

continued **Brown, D. N.**

1971   "Ethnomusicology and the Prehistoric Southwest." *Ethnomusicology* 15/no. 3:363-378.

1974   "Evidence for Dance from the Prehistoric Southwest." *CORD Research Annual* 6:263-284.

Brown, H.

1906   "A Pima-Maricopa Ceremony." *American Anthropologist* 8:689-690.

Bunzel, R.

1932   *Introduction to Zuni Ceremonialism.* Forty-seventh Annual Report, Bureau of American Ethnology.

Buttree, J. M.

1930   *The Rhythm of the Redman.* New York: A. S. Barnes and Company.

Carrithers, M.

1971   *Raids on the Squaw Dance: Some Sketches.* Unpublished M. A. thesis, Wesleyan University.

Cazeneuve, J.

1955   "Some Observations on Zuni Shalako." *El Palacio* 62:347-356.

Chapman, K. M.

1925   "Sun Basket Dance at Santa Clara." *El Palacio* 18:45-47.

1927   'The Shalako Ceremony at Zuni." *El Palacio* 23:622-627.

Chauvenet, B.

1929   "A Zuni Shalako." *El Palacio* 27:299-306.

Chesky, J.

1941   "Indian Music of the Southwest." *Kiva* 7:9-12.

Chiao, C.

1971   *Continuation of Tradition in Navajo Society.* Taipei: Institute of Ethnology, Academia Sinica, Monograph Series B, no. 3.

Clark, L. H.

1966   *They Sang for Horses: Impact of the Horse on Navajo and Apache Folklore.* Tucson: University of Arizona.

Collaer, P., ed.

1973   *Music of the Americas.* New York: Praeger Publishers.

Collins, J. J.

1968   "A Descriptive Introduction to the Taos Peyote Ceremony." *Ethnology* 7:427-449.

Colton, H. S., & E. Nequatewa

1932   *The Ladder Dance.* Museum of Northern Arizona, Museum Notes 5:4-12.

Committee on Research in Dance

1974   "New Dimensions in Dance Research: Anthropology and Dance—The American Indian." *CORD Research Annual,* vol. 6.

Crawford, D. E.

1967   "The Jesuit Relations and Allied Documents: Early Sources for an Ethnography of Music Among American Indians." *Ethnomusicology* 11/no. 2:199-206.

Curtis, E.

1907-1930   *The North American Indian.* Cambridge: University Press.

Curtis, N.

1904   "A Bit of American Folk Music: Two Pueblo Indian Grinding Songs." *Craftsman* 7:35-41.

1906   "Isleta: Hunting Song." *Southern Workman* 35:144.

1907   *The Indians Book.* New York: Harper and Brothers.

1921   "American Indian Cradle Songs." *Musical Quarterly* 7:549-558.

Davis, E. H.

1920   *The Papago Ceremony of Vikitia.* Heye Foundation, Indian Notes and Monographs 3:155-177.

De Huff, E.

1924   *From Desert and Pueblo: Five Authentic Navajo and Tewa Songs.* Boston, Massachusetts.

Dellenbaugh, F. S.

1915   "The Somaikoli Dance at Sichumovi." *American Museum Journal* 15:256-258.

Densmore, F.

1906   "Geronimo's Song." *Indian School Journal* 6/no. 6:30-31.

1921   "Music of the Papago and Pawnee." In *Explorations and Field-Work of the Smithsonian Institution in 1920*, pp. 102-107. Washington: Smithsonian Institution.

1926   "Poems from Desert Indians." *Nation* 122:407.

1927a   "Desert Indian Rain Chant." *World Review* 5:151.

1927b   "Study of Indian Music in the Nineteenth Century." *American Anthropologist* 29:77-86.

1929   *Papago Music.* Bureau of American Ethnology, Bulletin 90:1-230.

1931a   "Music of the Winnebago, Chippewa and Pueblo Indians." In *Explorations and Field-Work of the Smithsonian Institution in 1930*, pp. 217-224. Washington: Smithsonian Institution.

1931b   "Music of American Indians at Public Gatherings." *Musical Quarterly* 17:464-479.

1932a   "Resemblance Between Yuman and Pueblo Songs." *American Anthropologist* 34:694-700.

1932b   *Yuman and Yaqui Music.* Bureau of American Ethnology, Bulletin 110:1-216.

1938a   "Influence of Hymns on Forms of Indian Songs." *American Anthropologist* 40:175-177.

1938b   *Music of Santo Domingo Pueblo.* Southwest Museum Papers, no. 12, pp. 1-186.

1941   "Native Songs of Two Hybrid Ceremonies Among the American Indians." *American Anthropologist* 43:77-82.

1943   "Use of Meaningless Syllables in Indian Songs." *American Anthropologist* 45:160-162.

1944   "Traces of Foreign Influences in the Music of the American Indians." *American Anthropologist* 46:106-112.

1945   "Importance of Recordings of Indian Songs." *American Anthropologist* 47:637-639.

1947   "Imitative Dances Among the American Indians." *Journal of American Folklore* 60:73-78.

1950   "Words of Indian Songs as Unwritten Literature." *Journal of American Folklore* 63:450-458.

1953   "Use of Indian Music." *Musical America* 73/no. 5:15.

1954a   "Importance of Rhythm in Songs for the Treatment of the Sick by American Indians." *Scientific Monthly* 79:109-112.

1954b   "Music of the American Indian." *Southern Folklore Quarterly* 18:133-156.

1957a   "Music of the Indians in Our Western States." *Journal of American Folklore* 70:176-178.

1957b   *Music of Acoma, Isleta, Cochiti, and Zuni Pueblos.* Bureau of American Ethnology, Bulletin 165.

Di Peso, C.

1956   *The Upper Pima of San Cayetano del Tumacacori: An Archaeohistorical Reconstruction of the Ootam of Pimeria Alta.* Dragoon, Arizona.

Dockstader, F. J.

1953   "Origin of the Shalako." *Desert Magazine* 16/no. 1:29-30.

1957   *The American Indian in Graduate Studies. A Bibliography of Theses and Dissertations.* Heye Foundation, Contributions from the Museum of the American Indian, no. 15.

Dorsey, G. A., & H. R. Voth

1901   *The Oraibi Soyal Ceremony.* Field Museum, Anthropological Series 3:5-59.

1902   *The Mishongnovi Ceremonies of the Snake and Antelope Fraternities.* Field Museum, Anthropological Series 3:165-261.

Downey, J. C.

1970   "Review Essay of A. Lomax, Folk Song Style and Culture." *Ethnomusicology* 14/no. 1:63-67.

Draper, W. H.

1901   "Indian Dances of the Southwest." *Outing* 37:659-666.

Driver, H.

1970   "Review Essay of A. Lomax, Folk Song Style and Culture." *Ethnomusicology* 14/no. 1:57-62.

Dutton, B. P.

1936   "Hopi Dance of the Jemez Indians." *Research* 1:70-84.

1955   "Pueblo Fiestas, Navaho Ceremonies, Apache Ceremonies." In *New Mexico Indians and Their Arizona Neighbors,* pp. 11-16, 22-27, 33-35. Santa Fe: New Mexico Association on Indian Affairs.

1975   *Indians of the American Southwest.* Englewood Cliffs, N.J.: Prentice-Hall, Inc.

Espinosa, A. M.

1918   "All Souls' Day at Zuni, Acoma and Laguna." *Journal of American Folklore* 31:550-552.

Evans, B., & M. Evans

1931   *American Indian Dance Steps.* New York: A. S. Barnes and Company.

Farrer, C. R.

1976   *Mescalero Dance–A Four-Part Fugue.* Paper presented in the "Forms and Performance in Culture" Session, American Folklore Society Annual Meeting, November 11-14, Philadelphia.

Fay, C. E.

1952   "Some Notes on the Cow Dance, Santa Clara Pueblo." *El Palacio* 59:186-188.

Feder, N.

1962   "Matachines, a Photo Essay." *American Indian Tradition* 8/no. 2:79-82.

Ferguson, E.

1931   *Dancing Gods.* Albuquerque: University of New Mexico Press.

Fewkes, J. W.

1890a   "On the Use of the Phonograph Among Zuni Indians." *American Naturalist* 24:687-691.

1890b   "Additional Studies of Zuni Songs and Rituals with the Phonograph." *American Naturalist* 24:1094-1098.

1890c   *A Study of Summer Ceremonials at Zuni and Moqui Pueblos.* Bulletin of the Essex Institute 22/nos. 7-9:89-113.

1891a   "A Suggestion as to the Meaning of the Moki Snake Dance." *Journal of American Folklore* 4:129-138.

1891b   "A Few Summer Ceremonies at Zuni Pueblo." *Journal of American Ethnology and Archaeology* 1:1-61.

1893   "A Central American Ceremony which Suggests the Snake Dance of the Tusayan Villagers." *American Anthropologist* 6:285-306.

1894a   "The Walpi Flute Observance." *Journal of American Folklore* 7:265-287.

continued **Fewkes, J. W.**

1894b   "Snake Ceremonials at Walpi." *Journal of American Ethnology and Archaeology* 4/no. 1:1-126.

1895a   "The Oraibi Flute Altar." *Journal of American Folklore* 8:265-282.

1895b   "Provisional List of Annual Ceremonies at Walpi." *Internationales Archiv für Ethnographie* 8:215-238.

1895c   "A Comparison of Sia and Tusayan Snake Ceremonials." *American Anthropologist* 8:118-141.

1899   "Hopi Basket Dances." *Journal of American Folklore* 12:81-96.

1900   "The New Fire Ceremony at Walpi." *American Anthropologist* 2:80-138.

1901   "The Lesser New Fire Ceremony at Walpi." *American Anthropologist* 3:438-453.

1902   "Minor Hopi Festivals." *American Anthropologist* 4:482-511.

1910   "Butterfly Dance of the Hopi." In *The Butterfly in Hopi Myth and Ritual*, pp. 588-592. *American Anthropologist* 12:576-594.

Fewkes, J. W., & J. G. Owens

1892   "The Lā'-lā-Kōn-ta: A Tusayan Dance." *American Anthropologist* 5:105-129.

Fewkes, J. W., & A. M. Stephen

1892   "The Mam-Zrau'-ti: A Tusayan Ceremony." *American Anthropologist* 5:217-245.

Fillmore, J. G.

1896a   "Two Tigua Folk-Songs." *Land of Sunshine* 4:273-280.

1896b   "Songs of the Navajoes." *Land of Sunshine* 5:238-241.

1897   "Forms Spontaneously Assumed by Folk-songs." *Music* 12:289-294.

Fletcher, A. C.

1934   "Study of Indian Music." *American Anthropologist* 36:487-488.

Forde, C. D.

1931   *Ethnography of the Yuma Indians.* University of California Publications in American Archaeology and Ethnology 28/no. 4:83-278.

Forrest, E. R.

1961   *Snake Dance of the Hopi Indians.* Los Angeles: Westernlore Press.

Frisbie, C. J.

1967a   "Musical Instruments." In *An Analysis of the Worked Bone and Antler Artifacts from Sapawe, a P IV, Tewa Ruin in the Chama Valley,* pp. 51-73. Ms. 122 pp.

1967b   *Kinaaldá. A Study of the Navaho Girl's Puberty Ceremony.* Middletown: Wesleyan University Press.

1968   "The Navajo House Blessing Ceremony." *El Palacio* 75/no. 3:26-35.

1970   *The Navajo House Blessing Ceremony: A Study of Cultural Change.* Ph.D. dissertation, University of New Mexico. Ann Arbor: University Microfilms.

n.d.   "An Approach to the Ethnography of Navajo Ceremonial Performance." In *Ethnography of Performance,* edited by M. Herndon and N. McLeod. In Press. Ms. 1976.

Frisbie, C. J., & D. P. McAllester, eds.

n.d.   *Navajo Blessingway Singer. The Autobiography of Frank Mitchell, 1881–1967.* Tucson: University of Arizona Press. In Press. Ms. 1975.

Gallenkamp, C.

1954   "Raphael's Last Deer Dance." *Desert Magazine* 17/no. 5:11-14.

1955   "The Pueblo Indians of New Mexico." *Canadian Geographic Journal* 50:206-215.

Garcia, A., & C. Garcia

1968   "Ritual Preludes to Tewa Dances." *Ethnomusicology* 12/no. 1:239-244.

continued **Garcia, A., & C. Garcia**

1970   "Ritual Preludes and Postludes." In *Music and Dance of the Tewa Pueblos*, by G. Kurath, pp. 38-45. Museum of New Mexico Research Records, no. 8. Santa Fe: Museum of New Mexico Press.

Garcia, A., & J. and G. Trujillo

1966   "Tanoan Gestures of Invocation." *Ethnomusicology* 10/no. 2:206-207.

Gianini, C.

1928   "The Hopi Snake Dance." *El Palacio* 25:439-449.

Gifford, E.

1931   *The Southeastern Yavapai.* University of California Publications in American Archaeology and Ethnology 29:177-252.

Gill, S.

1974   *A Theory of Navajo Prayer Acts—A Study of Ritual Symbolism.* Unpublished Ph.D. dissertation, University of Chicago.

Gillis, F., & A. Merriam

1966   *Ethnomusicology and Folk Music: An International Bibliography of Dissertations and Theses.* Special Series in *Ethnomusicology*, no. 1. Middletown: Wesleyan University Press.

Gilman, B. I.

1891   "Zuni Melodies." *Journal of American Ethnology and Archaeology* 1:63-91.

1908   "Hopi Songs." *Journal of American Ethnology and Archaeology* 5:1-226.

Goldfrank, E.

1923   "Notes on Two Pueblo Feasts." *American Anthropologist* 25:188-196.

Gonzales, C.
  1966   "The Shalakos are Coming." *El Palacio* 73/no. 3:5-17.

Goodman, L.
  1968   *The Form and Function of the Basket Dance of San Juan Pueblo.*
        Unpublished M. A. thesis, Wesleyan University.

Goodwin, G.
  1942   *The Social Organization of the Western Apache.* Chicago: University of
        Chicago Press.

Gordon, D.
  1972   "An Early Fiesta at Laguna." *Masterkey* 46/no. 1:34-37.

Graham, S.
  1923   "The Shalaco Dance." *El Palacio* 15:139-140.

Griffith, J.
  1976   *Waila—The Contemporary Acculturative Dance Music of the Papago Indians.*
        Paper presented in the "Native American Folklore" Session, American
        Folklore Society Annual Meeting, November 11-14, Philadelphia.

Guernsey, S. J.
  1920   "Notes on a Navajo War Dance." *American Anthropologist* 22:304-307.

Haefer, R.
  1975   Personal Communications, March 10, April 3.

Hagemann, M.
  1893   *The Great Torture Chant of the Apaches . . . .* New York.

Haile, B. (O.F.M.)

1938 "Navaho Chantways and Ceremonials." *American Anthropologist* 40:639-652.

1946a *The Navaho Fire Dance or Corral Dance.* Saint Michaels, Arizona: Saint Michaels Mission Press.

1946b *The Navaho War Dance.* Saint Michaels, Arizona: Saint Michaels Mission Press.

Hall, T. B.

1953 "Dancing the Snakes." *Arizona Highways* 29/no. 7:4-11.

Harrington, J. P.

1908 "Yuma Account of Origins." *Journal of American Folklore* 21:324-348.

1912a "The Tewa Indian Game of Cañute." *American Anthropologist* 14:243-286.

1912b *The Devil Dance of the Apaches.* University of Pennsylvania, University Museum Journal, no. 3, pp. 6-10.

Harrington, J. P., & H. H. Roberts

1928 *Picuris Children's Stories with Texts and Songs.* Forty-third Annual Report, Bureau of American Ethnology, pp. 289-447.

Harrison, E.

1973 *Women in Navajo Myth. A Study in the Symbolism of Matriliny.* Unpublished Ph.D. dissertation, University of Massachusetts.

Harvey, B.

1966 "Song of the Dog Kachina." *Masterkey* 40/no. 3:106-108.

Hawley, F. E.

1937 "Kokopelli of the Prehistoric Southwestern Pueblo Pantheon." *American Anthropologist* 39:644-646.

1948 "Dance of the Devil Chasers." *New Mexico Magazine* 26/no. 9:16 et seq.

Hayden, J., & C. R. Steen

1937   *The Vikita Ceremony of the Papago.* Southwestern Monuments Monthly Reports, April, pp. 263-283. Coolidge.

Haywood, C.

1951   *A Bibliography of North American Folklore and Folksong.* New York: Greenberg Publishers.

Heizer, R. F.

1944   "The Hopi Snake Dance." *Ciba Symposium* 5:1681-1684.

Herzog, G.

1928   "The Yuman Musical Style." *Journal of American Folklore* 41:183-231.

1930   "Musical Styles in North America." *Proceedings of International Congress of Americanists* 23:455-458.

1931   "Transcriptions of Four Pueblo Melodies." In *American Indian Dance Steps,* by B. and M. Evans, pp. 54-56, 65-67. New York: A. S. Barnes and Company.

1933   "Maricopa Music." In *Yuman Tribes of the Gila River,* by L. Spier, pp. 271-279. Chicago: University of Chicago.

1934   "Speech Melody and Primitive Music." *Musical Quarterly* 20:452-466.

1935   "Special Song Types in North American Indian Music." *Zeitschrift für vergleichende Musikwissenschaft* 3:23-33.

1936a   *Research in Primitive and Folk Music in the United States.* American Council of Learned Societies Bulletin 24.

1936b   "A Comparison of Pueblo and Pima Musical Styles." *Journal of American Folklore* 49:283-417.

1947   "Some Linguistic Aspects of American Indian Poetry." *Word* 2:82-83.

Herndon, M.

1974   Personal Communication, October 24.

Heth, C.

1973   "Selected Bibliography on American Indian Music." *Music Library Association Newsletter* 14:2-4.

Hewett, E. L.

1918   "The Corn Ceremony at Santo Domingo." *El Palacio* 5:69-76.

Hickerson, J. C.

1961   *Annotated Bibliography of North American Indian Music North of Mexico.* Unpublished M. A. thesis, Indiana University.

Hieb, L.

1974   "Rhythms of Significance: Towards a Symbolic Analysis of Dance in Ritual." *CORD Research Annual* 6:225-233.

Hight, B.

1953   "Koyemshi: The Mudheads." *New Mexico Sun Trails* 6/no. 9:2-3.

Hill, G.

1954   *Bibliography of Pueblo Indian Dances and Ceremonies.* Santa Fe: Museum of New Mexico.

Hinton, L.

1974   Personal Communication, October 27.

Hinton, L., & D. Hanna

1971   "Havasupai Medicine Song." *Alcheringa* 3:68-75.

Hodge, F. W.

1896   "Pueblo Snake Ceremonials." *American Anthropologist* 9:133-136.

1920   *Hawikuh Bonework.* Heye Foundation, Indian Notes and Monographs, vol. 3, no. 3.

Hofmann, C.

1946   "Frances Densmore and the Music of the American Indians." *Journal of American Folklore* 59:45-50.

1972   *Musical Instruments of the Indians of the Americas.* Rochester, New York: Rochester Museum and Science Center.

Hood, M.

1971   *The Ethnomusicologist.* New York: McGraw-Hill.

Hough, W.

1897   "Music of the Hopi Flute Ceremony." *American Anthropologist* 10:162-163.

1899   *The Moki Snake Dance.* Chicago.

1915   "The Hopi Indians." *Little Histories of the North American Indians*, vol. 4.

1919   "The Hopi Indian Collection in the U.S. National Museum." *Proceedings of the U.S. National Museum* 54:235-296.

Hrdlička, A.

1905   "Notes on the San Carlos Apache." *American Anthropologist* 7:480-495.

1906   "Notes on Pima of Arizona." *American Anthropologist* 8:39-46.

Huebner, G.

1938   "The Green Corn Dance at Santo Domingo." *El Palacio* 45:1-17.

Hurt, W. R.

1952   "Christmas Eve Ceremonies of the Pueblo Indians of New Mexico." *Hobbies* 57:139.

1966   "The Spanish-American Comanche Dance." *Journal of Folklore Institute* 3/no. 2:116-132.

Jeancon, J. A.

1927   "Indian Music of the Southwest." *El Palacio* 23:438-447.

Johnson, C. I.

1964   "Navaho Corn Grinding Songs." *Ethnomusicology* 8/no. 2:101-120.

Johnson, J. B.

1940   "The Piman Foot Drum and Fertility Rites." *El Mexico Antiqua* 5:140-141.

Jones, A. W.

1937   *Additional Information about the Vikita.* Southwestern Monuments Monthly Reports, May, pp. 338-341. Coolidge.

Jones, H.

1931   "Zuni Shalako Ceremony." *El Palacio* 30:1-10.

1931b   "The Fiesta of San Geronimo at Taos." *El Palacio* 31:300-302.

1932   "Niman Katcina Dance at Walpi." *El Palacio* 33:68-71.

Joseph, A., R. Spicer, & J. Chesky

1949   *The Desert People: A Study of the Papago Indians.* Chicago: Chicago University Press.

Kanellos, V.

1953   "Prayer to Mother Earth." *New Mexico* 31/no. 4:18-19, 45.

1956   "Rituals in the Old Tradition." *New Mexico* 34/no. 12:24, 59.

Kealiinohomoku, J.

1967   "Hopi and Polynesian Dance: A Study in Cross-Cultural Comparisons." *Ethnomusicology* 11/no. 3:343-358.

1970a   "An Anthropologist Looks at Ballet as a Form of Ethnic Dance." In *Impulse 1969-1970,* edited by Marian Van Tuyl, pp. 24-33. San Francisco: Impulse Publications.

1970b   "Perspective Five: Ethnic Historical Study." In *Dance History Research: Perspectives from Related Arts and Disciplines,* edited by J. Kealiino-homoku, pp. 86-97. New York: Committee on Research in Dance.

| 1974a | "Field Guides." *CORD Research Annual* 6:245-260. |

1974b   "Dance Culture as a Microcosm of Holistic Culture." *CORD Research Annual* 6:99-106.

1974c   Personal Communication, November 4.

1975   Personal Communication, March 5.

Kealiinohomoku, J., & F. Gillis

1970   "Special Bibliography: G. P. Kurath." *Ethnomusicology* 14/no. 1: 114-128.

Keech, R. A.

1934a   "The Pecos Ceremony at Jemez August 2, 1932." *El Palacio* 36/nos. 17-18:129-135.

1934b   "Green Corn Ceremony at the Pueblo of Zia." *El Palacio* 36:145-149.

1937   "The Blue Corn Dance." *National Archaeological News* 1/no. 9:26-28.

Kidder, A. V.

1951   "Whistles from Arizona." *American Antiquity* 16:256.

King, B. M.

1935   *A Study of Form and Expression in American Indian Music as Exemplified in the Songs of Jemez Pueblo.* Unpublished M. A. thesis, University of Minnesota.

Klah, H.

1942   *Navajo Creation Myth.* Museum of Navajo Ceremonial Art, Navajo Religion Series, vol. 1. Santa Fe.

Klett, F.

1879   *The Cachina: A Dance at the Pueblo of Zuni.* Report upon U. S. Geographic Surveys West of the 100th Meridian 7:332-336.

Kluckhohn, C.

1923   "The Dance of Hasjelti." *El Palacio* 15:187-192.

1933   "Great Chants of the Navajo." *Theatre Arts Monthly* 17:639-645.

1938a   "Participation in Ceremonials in a Navaho Community." *American Anthropologist* 40:359-369.

1938b   "Navaho Women's Knowledge of Their Song Ceremonials." *El Palacio* 45:87-92.

Kluckhohn, C., & L. Wyman

1940   *An Introduction to Navaho Chant Practice.* Memoirs of the American Anthropological Association, no. 53.

Kolinski, M.

1972   "An Apache Rabbit Dance Song Cycle as Sung by the Iroquois." *Ethnomusicology* 16/no. 3:415-464.

Korson, R., & J. Hickerson

1969   "The Willard Rhodes Collection of American Indian Music in the Archive of Folk Song." *Ethnomusicology* 13/no. 2:296-304. "A Special Bibliography: Willard Rhodes" follows on pages 305-308.

Krader, B.

1956   "Bibliography of George Herzog." *Society for Ethnomusicology Newsletter*, no. 6, pp. 11-20 and no. 8, p. 10.

Kroeber, A. L., ed.

1935   *Walapai Ethnography.* Memoirs of the American Anthropological Association, no. 42.

Kroeber, H. R.

1909   "Papago Coyote Tales." *Journal of American Folklore* 22:339-342.

Kurath, G. P.

1950   "New Method of Choreographic Notation." *American Anthropologist* 52:120-123.

1953   "Native Choreographic Areas of North America." *American Anthropologist* 55:60-73.

1955   "Aboriginal American Folk Dance." *Folk Dancer* 2/no. 5:117-118.

1956a   "Choreography and Anthropology." *American Anthropologist* 58:177-179.

1956b   "Masked Clowns." *Tomorrow* 4/no. 3:108-112.

1957a   "Basic Techniques of Amerindian Dance." *Dance Notation Record* 8/no. 4: 2-8.

1957b   "Notation of a Pueblo Indian Corn Dance." *Dance Notation Record* 8/no. 4: 9-10.

1957c   "The Origin of the Pueblo Indian Matachines." *El Palacio* 64/nos. 9-10: 259-264.

1957d   "Dance Styles of the Rio Grande Pueblo Indians." *The Folklorist* 4/no. 3:89.

1958a   "Plaza Circuits of Tewa Indian Dancers." *El Palacio* 65/nos. 1-2:16-28.

1958b   "Two Line Dances of San Juan Pueblo, New Mexico." *Midwest Folklore* 8:155-158.

1958c   "Game Animal Dances of the Rio Grande Pueblos." *Southwestern Journal of Anthropology* 14/no. 4:438-448.

1958d   "Buffalo Dances at Cochiti Pueblo, New Mexico." *The Folklorist* 4/no. 5: 149-150.

1959   "Cochiti Choreographies and Songs." In *Cochiti,* by C. H. Lange, pp. 539-556. Austin: University of Texas Press.

1960a   "Panorama of Dance Ethnology." *Current Anthropology* 1/no. 3:233-254.

1960b   "Calling the Rain Gods." *Journal of American Folklore* 73:312-316.

1960c   "The Sena'asom Rattle of the Yaqui Indian Pascolas." *Ethnomusicology* 4/no. 2:60-63.

1961-1962   "American Indian Dance in Ritual and Life." *Folklorist* 6/nos. 4, 5, 6:428-435, 446-449, 479-482, and 7/nos. 1, 2, 3:8-11, 41-47, 70-77.

1963   "Tewa Plaza Dances, a Photo Essay." *American Indian Tradition* 9/no. 1: 16-21.

continued **Kurath, G. P.**

1965   "Tewa Choreographic Music." *Studies in Ethnomusicology,* edited by M. Kolinski, vol. 2, pp. 4-19. New York: Oak Publications.

1966a   "The Kinetic Ecology of Yaqui Dance Instrumentation." *Ethnomusicology* 10/no. 1:28-42.

1966b   "Review of One Folkways Record: Healing Songs of the American Indian." *Ethnomusicology* 10/no. 3:372.

1969   "A Comparison of Plains and Pueblo Songs." *Ethnomusicology* 13/no. 3: 512-517.

1974   "Music and Dance of American Indian Peoples." In *The Arts of American Indian Peoples,* Sections II and III, pp. 663-676. *Encyclopedia Britannica,* 15th ed., vol. 1, pp. 658-694.

Kurath, G. P. (with A. Garcia)

1970   *Music and Dance of the Tewa Pueblos.* Museum of New Mexico Research Records, no. 8. Santa Fe: Museum of New Mexico Press.

Lamphere, L.

1969   "Symbolic Elements in Navajo Ritual." *Southwestern Journal of Anthropology* 25:279-305.

Lange, C. H.

1951   "King's Day Ceremonies at a Rio Grande Pueblo, January 6, 1940." *El Palacio* 58/no. 12:398-406.

1952a   "San Juan's Day at Cochiti Pueblo, New Mexico, 1894 and 1947." *El Palacio* 69:175-182.

1952b   "The Feast Day Dance at Zia Pueblo." *Texas Journal of Science* 4:19-26.

1953   "Notes on a Winter Ceremony at Isleta Pueblo, January 7, 1940." *El Palacio* 60/no. 3:116-123.

1954   "An Animal Dance at Santo Domingo Pueblo, January 26, 1940." *El Palacio* 61/no. 5:151-155.

1957   "*Tablita* or Corn, Dances of the Rio Grande Pueblo Indians." *Texas Journal of Science* 9/no. 1:59-74.

1959   *Cochiti: A New Mexico Pueblo, Past and Present.* Austin: University of
             Texas Press.

1975   "A Time Capsule from the 1880s: Bandelier's 'Memoranda of Investigations
             Required.'" In *Collected Papers in Honor of Florence Hawley Ellis,* edited
             by T. R. Frisbie, pp. 224-245. Papers of the Archaeological Society of New
             Mexico, no. 2. Norman: Hooper Publishing Company.

Laski, V.

1957   "The Raingod Ceremony of the Tewa, a Religious Drama." *Masterkey*
             31/no. 3:76-84.

La Vigna, M.

1976   *The San Juan Pueblo Turtle Dance: A Guide to the Past, Present, and
             Future.* Paper presented in the "Music of the First Americans" Session,
             21st Annual Meeting of the Society for Ethnomusicology, November
             10-14, Philadelphia.

Lawrence, D. H.

1934   "Indianische Mysterien: der tanz des spriessenden Korns; der schlangentanz
             der Hopi-Indianer." *Neue Rundschan* 45/no. 1:79-94.

Lea, H.

1953   "The Basket Dance." *New Mexico* 31/no. 5:18, 55.

1954   "Prayer to the Sun." *New Mexico* 32/no. 3:22, 37.

1963-1964   "More About the Matachines." *New Mexoco Folklore Record* 11:7-10.

Lehmer, D. M.

1929   "Music and Poetry of American Indians." *Poetry Review* 20:333-340.

Lewis, O. L.

1953   "Fiesta at Nambe Pueblo." *El Palacio* 60/no. 12:409-413.

Link, M. S.

1960   "From the Desk of Washington Matthews." *Journal of American Folklore* 73:317-325.

List, G.

1962   "Songs in Hopi Culture, Past and Present." *Journal of International Folk Music Council* 14:30-35.

1963   "The Boundaries of Speech and Song." *Ethnomusicology* 7:1-16.

1964   "The Hopi and White Man's Music." *Sing Out* 14/no. 2:47-49.

1966   "Review of One Folkways Record: Hopi Katcina Songs and Six Other Songs by Hopi Chanters." *Ethnomusicology* 10/no. 3:373.

1968   "Hopi as Composer and Poet." In *Proceedings of Centennial Workshop in Ethnomusicology*, University of British Columbia, Vancouver, June 19-23, 1967, edited by P. Crossley Holland, 1970, 3rd ed., pp. 43-53.

Litvinoff, V.

1973   "Yaqui Easter." *Drama Review* 17:52-63.

1974   "Lessons from the Dancing Ground to the Studio: Implications of Pueblo Indian Dance for Modern Dance." *Journal of Aesthetics and Art Criticism* 32/no. 3:394-407.

Lloyd, E.

1940   *The Papago Feast of Saint Francis.* Southwestern Monuments Monthly Reports, pp. 389-392. Coolidge.

Lomax, A.

1959   "Folk Song Style." *American Anthropologist* 61:927-954.

1962   "Song Structure and Social Structure." *Ethnology* 1/no. 4:425-451.

1968   *Folk Song Style and Culture.* American Association for Advancement of Science Publication, no. 88. Washington.

Lomax, A., I. Bartenieff, & P. Paulay

1974   "Choreometrics: A Method for the Study of Cross-Cultural Pattern in Film." *CORD Research Annual* 6:193-212.

Longacre, W.

1973   "Current Directions in Southwestern Archaeology." In *Annual Review of Anthropology*, edited by B. Siegel, no. 2, pp. 201-220. Palo Alto: California: Annual Reviews, Inc.

Lowie, R.

1938   "The Emergence Hole and the Foot Drum." *American Anthropologist* 40:174.

Lujan, E., & J. Lujan

1962   "The Hoop Dance." *New Mexico Magazine* 40/nos. 11-12:37, 39.

MacLeish, K.

1941   "A Few Hopi Songs from Moenkopi." *Masterkey* 15:178-184.

Marshall, L. R.

1941   "A Drum for the Navajo Chorus." *Etude* 59:126.

Mason, J. A.

1920   "Papago Harvest Festival." *American Anthropologist* 22:13-25.

Mason, O. T.

1897   "Geographical Distribution of the Musical Bow." *American Anthropologist* 10:377-380.

Matthews, W.

1887   *The Mountain Chant: A Navajo Ceremony.* Fifth Annual Report, Bureau of American Ethnology.

1889   "Navaho Gambling Songs." *American Anthropologist* 2:1-19.

1894a   "The Basket Drum." *American Anthropologist* 7:202-208.

continued **Matthews, W.**

1894b "Songs of Sequence of the Navajos." *Journal of American Folklore* 7:185-194.

1896 "Songs of the Navajos." *Land of Sunshine* 5:197-201.

1897 *Navaho Legends.* Memoirs of the American Folklore Society, no. 5, pp. 1-300.

1902 "The Night Chant." *Memoirs of American Museum of Natural History* 6:1-332.

McAllester, D. P.

1949 *Peyote Music.* Viking Fund Publications in Anthropology, no. 13. New York: Viking Fund, Inc.

1952 *Navajo Creation Chants.* Pamphlet to accompany Album of 5 Records produced by Peabody Museum, Harvard University.

1954 *Enemyway Music.* Papers of the Peabody Museum of American Archaeology and Ethnology, Harvard University, vol. 41, no. 3.

1955 "American Indian Songs and Pan Tribalism." *Midwest Folklore* 5:132-136.

1956a "The Role of Music in Western Apache Culture." In *Selected Papers of the Fifth International Congress of Anthropological and Ethnological Sciences,* September 1-9, Philadelphia, pp. 468-472.

1956b *Myth and Prayers of the Great Star Chant and the Myth of the Coyote Chant.* Editor and author of commentaries on material recorded by Mary C. Wheelwright. Museum of Navajo Ceremonial Art, Navajo Religion Series. Santa Fe.

1956c "An Apache Fiddle." *Society for Ethnomusicology Newsletter,* no. 8, pp. 1-5.

1961 *Indian Music in the Southwest.* Colorado Springs: Taylor Museum.

1958 "Review of Two Canyon Records: Navajo: Songs of the Diné, and Apache: Songs by Philip and Patsy Cassadore of the San Carlos Tribe." *Ethnomusicology* 12/no. 3:470-473.

1969 "Review of Indian House Record: Navajo Sway Songs." *Ethnomusicology* 13/no. 2:401-403.

1970   "Blessingway Songs." In *Blessingway,* by L. Wyman, pp. 177-194. Tucson: University of Arizona.

1971a   "Review of Two Canyon Records and One Indian House Recording: Memories of Navajoland, sung by Ed Lee Natay; Philip Cassadore Sings Apache Songs; and Night and Daylight Yeibichai, sung by Navaho singers from Klagetoh, Arizona–leader, Boniface Bonnie." *Ethnomusicology* 15/no. 1:164-170.

1971b   "Review of One Indian House Record: Navajo Skip Dance and Two-Step Songs." *Ethnomusicology* 15/no. 2:296-297.

1971c   *Readings in Ethnomusicology.* New York: Johnson Reprint Corporation.

1972   "Review of Music and Dance of the Tewa Pueblos," by G. P. Kurath. *Ethnomusicology* 16/no. 3:546-547.

n.d.   "The First Snake Songs." In *Collected Papers in Honor of Gene Weltfish,* edited by S. Diamond. In Press. Ms. 1976.

McAllester, D. P., & D. Brown

1962   *Music of the Pueblos, Apache and Navaho.* LP Record and Booklet. Colorado Springs: Taylor Museum.

McAllester, D. P., & D. Mitchell

n.d.   "Navajo Music." In *Handbook of North American Indians,* volume edited by A. Ortiz, vol. 9, pt. 2 (The Southwest). In Press. Ms. 1972.

McElvary, M. F.

1951   "The Deer Dance at Christmas." *New Mexico* 29/no. 12:13, 34-35.

1953   "Shepherd's Fires." *New Mexico* 31/no. 12:21, 33.

McLeod, N.

1974   "Ethnomusicological Research and Anthropology." In *Annual Review of Anthropology,* edited by B. Siegel, no. 2, pp. 99-115. Palo Alto: California: Annual Reviews, Inc.

Mead, M.

1959   *An Anthropologist at Work: Writings of Ruth Benedict.* Boston: Houghton Mifflin Company.

Mead, S. M., & J. E. Mead

1968-1969   "The Southwest, U.S.A.: The Indians and Some of Their Dances." *Te Ao How* 65:10-12. (Wellington, New Zealand)

Merriam, A.

1964a   *The Anthropology of Music.* Evanston: Northwestern University Press.

1964b   "The Arts and Anthropology." In *Horizons of Anthropology*, edited by S. Tax, pp. 224-236. Chicago: Aldine.

1966   "The Anthropology of Music." Current Anthropology Book Review with Comments. *Current Anthropology* 7/no. 2:217-230.

1974   "Anthropology and the Dance." *CORD Research Annual* 6:9-27.

Michener, B.

1966a   "Yei-be-chai." *Viltis* 25/no. 1:20-21.

1966b   "The Fire Dance." *Viltis* 25/no. 2:7-9.

Miles, C.

1953   "Aboriginal Musical Instruments in North America." *Hobbies* 57:134-137.

Miller, J.

1975   "Kokopelli." In *Collected Papers in Honor of Florence Hawley Ellis*, edited by T. R. Frisbie, pp. 371-380. Papers of the Archaeological Society of New Mexico, no. 2. Norman: Hooper Publishing Company.

Mindeleff, C.

1886   "An Indian Dance." *Science* 7:507-514.

1898   *Navaho Houses.* Seventeenth Annual Report, Bureau of American Ethnology, pt. 2, pp. 469-517.

Montell, G.

  1938   "Yaqui Dances." *Ethnos* 3/no. 6:145-166.

Morris, E. A.

  1959   "Basketmaker Flutes from Prayer Rock District, Arizona." *American Antiquity* 24:406-411.

Moskowitz, I., & J. Collier

  1949   *Patterns and Ceremonials of the Indians of the Southwest.* New York: E. P. Dutton and Co., Inc.

  1972   *American Indian Ceremonial Dances.* New York: Bounty. (Originally published as *Patterns and Ceremonials of the Indians of the Southwest.*)

Music Educators Journal

  1972   *Music in World Cultures.* (October)

Nettl, B.

  1953a   "Review of Three LP's by Densmore and the Library of Congress." *Midwest Folklore* 3:124-125.

  1953b   "Observations on Meaningless Peyote Song Texts." *Journal of American Folklore* 66:161-164.

  1953c   "Stylistic Variety in North American Indian Music." *Journal of American Musicological Society* 6:160-168.

  1954   *North American Indian Musical Styles.* Memoirs of the American Folklore Society, no. 45.

  1955   "Musicological Studies in American Ethnological Journals." *Music Library Association Notes* 12:205-209.

  1956   *Music in Primitive Culture.* Cambridge: Harvard University Press.

  1959   "Review of Densmore's Music of Acoma, Isleta, Cochiti and Zuni Pueblos." *Ethnomusicology* 3/no. 1:34-35.

  1960   *An Introduction to Folk Music in the United States.* Wayne State University Studies, no. 7. Detroit: Wayne State University Press.

continued **Nettl, B.**

1961   "Polyphony in North American Indian Music." *Musical Quarterly* 47: 354-362.

1964   *Theory and Method in Ethnomusicology.* New York: Free Press of Glencoe.

1965   *Folk and Traditional Music of the Western Continents.* 2nd ed., 1973. Englewood Cliffs, N.J.: Prentice Hall.

1966   "Some Influences of Western Civilization on North American Music." In *New Voices in American Studies,* edited by R. Browne, D. Winkelman, and A. Hayman, pp. 129-137. Lafayette, Indiana: Purdue University Studies.

1969   "Musical Areas Reconsidered; A Critique of North American Indian Research." In *Essays in Musicology in Honor of Dragan Plamenac on His 70th Birthday,* pp. 181-189. Pittsburgh: University of Pittsburgh Press.

1970   "Review of A. Lomax's Folk Song Style and Culture." *American Anthropologist* 72:438-441.

1975   "The Western Impact on World Music: Africa and American Indians." In *Contemporary Music and Music Cultures,* edited by C. Hamm, B. Nettl, and R. Byrnside, pp. 101-124. Englewood Cliffs, N.J.: Prentice-Hall, Inc.

Nequatewa, E.

1946   "The Flute Ceremony at Hotevilla." *Plateau* 19:35-36.

Nicholas, D.

1939   "Mescalero Apache Girl's Puberty Ceremony." *El Palacio* 46:193-204.

Nicholson, H. S.

1945   *Four Songs from a Yuma Version of Los Pastores.* University of Arizona General Bulletin 9:25-28.

Oakden, E. C., & M. Sturt

1927   "The Snake Dance of the Hopi Indians." *Scottish Geographical Magazine* 43:41-44.

Oliver, M. L.

    1911   "The Snake Dance." *National Geographic Magazine* 22/no. 2:107-137.

Opler, M. E.

    1941   *An Apache Life-Way.* Chicago: University of Chicago Press.

    1968   "Remuneration to Supernaturals and Man in Apachean Ceremonialism." *Ethnology* 7:356-393.

    1969   "Western Apache and Kiowa Apache Materials Relating to Ceremonial Payment." *Ethnology* 8:122-124.

Ortiz, A.

    1969a   *The Tewa World.* Chicago: University of Chicago Press.

    1969b   "Review of One Taos Recordings and Publications' Record: So These Won't Be Forgotten: Music of Picuris Pueblo, New Mexico." *Ethnomusicology* 13/no. 3:586-588.

Painter, M. T.

    1974   "A Yaqui Easter." *CORD Research Annual* 6:347-350.

Pancoast, C. L.

    1918   "Last Dance of the Picuris." *National History* 18:308-311.

Parsons, E. C.

    1917   "All-Souls' Day at Zuni, Acoma and Laguna." *Journal of American Folklore* 30:495-496.

    1919   "Note on a Navajo War Dance." *American Anthropologist* 21:465-467.

    1921   "Note on the Night Chant at Tuwelchedu." *American Anthropologist* 23:240-243.

    1922a   *Winter and Summer Dance Series in Zuni.* University of California Publications in American Archaeology and Ethnology 17:171-216.

    1922b   "Ceremonial Dances at Zuni." *El Palacio* 13:119-122.

continued **Parsons, E. C.**

1923a "The Hopi Buffalo Dance." *Man* 23:21-27.

1923b "Fiesta at Sant' Ana." *Scientific Monthly* 16:178-183.

1924 *The Scalp Ceremonial of Zuni.* Memoirs of the American Anthropological Association, no. 31, pp. 1-42.

1938 "Humpbacked Flute Player of the Southwest." *American Anthropologist* 40:337-338.

1939 *Pueblo Indian Religion.* 2 vols. Chicago: University of Chicago Press.

Parsons, McIlvaine

1926 "The San Juan Turtle Dance." *Horae Scholasticae* 59:177-179.

Peabody, C.

1917 "A Prehistoric Wind-Instrument from Pecos, New Mexico." *American Anthropologist* 19:30-33.

Pilling, A.

1962 "Some Questions on Taos Dancing." *Ethnomusicology* 6/no. 2:88-92.

Pillsbury, D. L.

1952 "Christmas Eve in San Felipe." *Desert Magazine* 15/no. 12:22-24.

Raymond, J.

1960-1961 "Kumanche of the Zuni Indians of New Mexico." *Folklorist* 6/no. 3: 400-402.

Reagan, A. B.

1906 "Dances of the Jemez Pueblo Indians." *Transactions of the Kansas Academy of Science* 23:241-272.

1914   *Don Diego or the Pueblo Uprising of 1680.* New York: Harriman.

1915a   "The Masked Dance of the Jemez Indians." *Southern Workman* 44:
            423-427.

1915b   "The Corn Dance at Jemez." *Southern Workman* 44:481-484.

1929   "Fourth of July Summer Solstice Ceremony of the Navajos." *Southern
            Workman* 58:310-313.

1934   "A Navaho Fire Dance." *American Anthropologist* 36:434-437.

Reichard, G.

1934   *Spider Woman.* New York: MacMillan.

1939   *Dezba.* New York: J. J. Augustin.

1950   *Navaho Religion.* 2 vols. New York: Bollingen Foundation.

Reilly, P. T.

1970   "The Disappearing Havasupai Corn-planting Ceremony." *Masterkey* 44/
            no. 1:30-34.

Rexroth, K.

1956   "American Indian Songs: U.S. Bureau of Ethnology Collection."
            Perspectives U.S.A. 16:197-201.

Reyman, J.

1974   *Evidence for the Influence of Natural Rhythms in Southwestern Pueblo
            Dance Patterns.* Paper presented at 19th Annual Meeting of Society for
            Ethnomusicology, held jointly with Committee on Research in Dance,
            October 24-27, San Francisco.

Rhodes, R. W.

1973   *Selected Hopi Secular Music.* Unpublished Ph.D. dissertation, Arizona
            State University.

Rhodes, W.

1952a   "Acculturation in North American Indian Music." In *Acculturation in the Americas.* Proceedings and Selected Papers of the Twenty-ninth International Congress of Americanists, edited by S. Tax, Vol. II, pp. 127-132. New York: Cooper Square Publishers.

1952b   "North American Indian Music: A Bibliographic Survey of Anthropological Theory." *Music Library Association Notes* 10:33-45.

1956a   "American Indian Music." *Tomorrow* 4:97-102.

1956b   "Bibliography of Frances Densmore," with Introduction. *Society for Ethnomusicology Newsletter,* no. 7, April, pp. 13-29.

1963   "North American Indian Music in Transition." *Journal of International Folk Music Council* 15:9-14.

1967   "Special Bibliography: Helen Heffron Roberts." *Ethnomusicology* 14/no. 1:114-128.

Risner, V.

1973   *Dance Ethnography Data Inventory.* Los Angeles: University of California at Los Angeles, Department of Dance.

Robb, J. D.

1952-1953   "The J. D. Robb Collection of Folk Music Recordings." *New Mexico Folklore* 7:6-20.

1961   "The Matachines Dance—A Ritual Folk Dance." *Western Folklore* 20/no. 2: 87-101.

1964   "Rhythmic Patterns of the Santo Domingo Corn Dance." *Ethnomusicology* 8/no. 2:154-160.

Roberts, D. L.

1964   "A Brief Guide to Rio Grande Pueblo Dances." *Quarterly of the Southwestern Association on Indian Affairs* 1/no. 2:12-15.

1965   "Review of Six Taos Recordings and Publications' Records: Taos Indian Songs, Taos Spanish Songs, New Mexican Alabados, Taos Matachines Music, Picuris Indian Songs, and Bailes de Taos. *Ethnomusicology* 9/no. 2: 205-206.

1970   "Tewa Pueblo Round Dances." In *Music and Dance of the Tewa Pueblos*, by G. Kurath. Museum of New Mexico Research Records, no. 8, pp. 292-302. Santa Fe: Museum of New Mexico Press.

1972   "The Ethnomusicology of the Eastern Pueblos." In *New Perspectives on the Pueblos*, edited by A. Ortiz, pp. 243-256. Albuquerque: University of New Mexico Press.

Roberts, H. H.

1923   "Chakwena Songs of Zuni and Laguna." *Journal of American Folklore* 36:177-184.

1927   "Indian Music from the Southwest." *Natural History* 27:257-265.

1936   *Musical Areas in Aboriginal North America.* Yale University Publications in Anthropology, no. 12.

Roeder, L. E.

1953   "The Matachines at Jemez Pueblo." *New Mexico Sun Trails* 6/no. 5:121.

Roediger, V.

1961   *Ceremonial Costumes of the Pueblo Indians.* Berkeley: University of California Press.

Rothenberg, J.

1972   *Shaking the Pumpkin.* New York: Doubleday.

Russell, F.

1898   "An Apache Medicine Dance." *American Anthropologist* 11:367-372.

1908   *The Pima.* Twenty-sixth Annual Report, Bureau of American Ethnology, pp. 3-389.

Rust, H. N.

1896   "The Moqui Snake Dance." *Land of Sunshine* 4:70-76.

Sachs, C.

    1937   *World History of the Dance.* New York: W. W. Norton and Company.

    1940   *The History of Musical Instruments.* New York: W. W. Norton and Company.

Schevill, M.

    1947   *Beautiful on the Earth.* Tucson: University of Arizona Press.

Schweitzer, J., & R. K. Thomas

    1952   "Fiesta of St. Francis at San Francisquito, Sonora." *Kiva* 18/nos. 1-2:1-7.

Seder, T.

    1952   *Old World Overtones in the New World: Some Parallels with North American Musical Instruments.* University of Pennsylvania, University Museum Bulletin, no. 16, p. 4.

Sloane, E.

    1962   "Hoop Dance." *New Mexico Magazine* 40/nos. 11-12:39.

Smith, H. E.

    1971   "Southwestern Studies—A View to the Future." *Human Organization* 30:427-436.

Smithson, C. L.

    1959   *The Havasupai Woman.* University of Utah Anthropological Papers, no. 38.

Snyder, A. F.

    1966   "Navajo Night Dances and Ballet's Golden Age." *Film News* 23/no. 5: 12.

1974   "The Dance Symbol." *CORD Research Annual* 6:213-224.

Spicer, E. H.

1940   *Pascua: A Yaqui Village in Arizona.* Chicago: University of Chicago Press.

1974   "Context of the Yaqui Easter Ceremony." *CORD Research Annual* 6: 309-346.

Spier, L.

1928   *Havasupai Ethnography.* American Museum of Natural History, Anthropological Papers 29/no. 3:81-392.

Spinden, H. J.

1915a   "Home Songs of the Tewa Indians." *American Museum Journal* 15:73-78.

1915b   "Indian Dances of the Southwest." *American Museum Journal* 15:103-115.

1933   *Songs of the Tewa.* New York.

Stacey, R.

1907   "Some Zuni Ceremonies and Melodies." *Music Lover's Calendar* 2:54-61.

Stephen, A. M.

1936   *Hopi Journal,* edited by E. C. Parsons. New York: Columbia University Press.

1937   "Clowns in Hopi Ceremonial Dances." *Nature* 139:888.

1939-1940   "The Hopi Indians of Arizona." *Masterkey* 13 and 14.

Sterling, M. W.

1941   *Snake Bites and the Hopi Snake Dance.* Annual Reports, Bureau of Regents, Smithsonian Institution, pp. 551-555.

Stevenson, M. C.

1894   *The Sia.* Eleventh Annual Report, Bureau of American Ethnology, pp. 3-157.

continued **Stevenson, M. C.**

    1904   *The Zuni Indians.* Twenty-third Annual Report, Bureau of American Ethnology.

Stevenson, R.

    1973a   "Written Sources for Indian Music until 1882." *Ethnomusicology* 17/no. 1:1-40.

    1973b   "English Sources for Indian Music until 1882." *Ethnomusicology* 17/no. 3:399-442.

Stricklen, E. G.

    1923   *Notes on Eight Papago Songs.* University of California Publications in American Archaeology and Ethnology 20:361-366.

Sweet, J.

    1976   *Time, Space and Festival: An Analysis of a Tewa Indian Event.* Paper presented in the "Anthropology and Dance" Session, 5th Annual CORD Conference, November 11-14, Philadelphia.

Taylor, B.

    1974   "The Physical Values and Physiological Function of American Indian Dance." *CORD Research Annual* 6:149-165.

Tedlock, B. J.

    1973   *Kachina Dance Songs in Zuni Society: The Role of Aesthetics in Social Integration.* Unpublished M. A. thesis, Wesleyan University.

Tedlock, D.

    1972   *Finding the Center: Narrative Poetry of Zuni Indians.* New York: Dial Press.

Thompson, G.

    1889   "An Indian Dance at Jemez." *American Anthropologist* 2:351-355.

Tress, A.

1968   "Deer Dances I Have Seen." *Dance Magazine* 42/no. 9:58-61, 84-85.

Troyer, C.

1913   *The Zuni Indians and Their Music.* Philadelphia: Theodore Presser Company.

Underhill, R. M.

1938   *Singing for Power: The Song Magic of the Papago Indians.* Berkeley: University of California.

Valenzuela, J.

1974   "Roots, Branches, and Blossoms." *CORD Research Annual* 6:299-306.

Van Stone, M. R.

1941   "Songs of the Indians." *El Palacio* 48:149-154.

Voegelin, C. F., & R. C. Euler

1957   "Introduction to Hopi Chants." *Journal of American Folklore* 70:115-136.

Vogt, E. Z.

1955   "Study of the Southwestern Fiesta System as Exemplified by the Laguna Fiesta." *American Anthropologist* 57:820-839.

Voth, H. R.

1901   *Oraibi Powamu Ceremony.* Field Museum, Anthropological Series 3:67-158.

1903a   *Oraibi Oáqol Ceremony.* Field Museum, Anthropological Series 6:1-46.

1903b   *Oraibi Summer Snake Ceremonies.* Field Museum, Anthropological Series 3:267-358.

1912a   *Oraibi Marau.* Field Museum, Anthropological Series 11:1-88.

continued **Voth, H. R.**

1912b   *Oraibi New Year Ceremony.* Field Museum, Anthropological Series 11: 111-119.

1912c   *Tewa Baholawu of the Oraibi Flute Societies.* Field Museum, Anthropological Series 11:121-136.

Wagner, R.

1975a   "Pattern and Process in Ritual Syncretism: The Case of Peyotism Among the Navajo." *Journal of Anthropological Research* 31/no. 2:162-181.

1975b   "Some Pragmatic Aspects of Navaho Peyotism." *Plains Anthropologist* 20/no. 69:197-205.

Walton, E. L.

1926   *Dawn Boy: Blackfoot and Navaho Songs.* New York: Dutton and Company.

1930   "Navajo Song Patterning." *Journal of American Folklore* 43:105-118.

Ware, N.

1970   "Survival and Change in Pima Indian Music." *Ethnomusicology* 14/no. 1: 100-113.

Weinman, J.

1970   "The Influence of Pueblo Worldview on the Construction of its Vocal Music." *Ethnomusicology* 14/no. 2:313-315.

White, L.

1935   *The Pueblo of Santo Domingo, New Mexico.* Memoirs of the American Anthropological Association, no. 43.

1942   *The Pueblo of Santa Ana, New Mexico.* Memoirs of the American Anthropological Association, no. 60.

Whitman, W.

1947   *The Pueblo Indians of San Ildefonso.* Columbia University Contributions to Anthropology, no. 34.

Wilder, C. S.

1963   *The Yaqui Deer Dance: A Study in Cultural Change.* Bureau of American Ethnology, Bulletin 186:145-210.

Williamson, G., et al.

1950   "The Fiesta of Saint Francis Xavier." *Kiva,* vol. 16, nos. 1-2.

Witherspoon, G.

1975   *Navajo Kinship and Marriage.* Chicago: University of Chicago Press.

Woodward, A.

1937   "A Song of the Navaho War." *Masterkey* 11/no. 1:26-28.

Wyman, L.

1962   *The Windways of the Navaho.* Colorado Springs: Taylor Museum.

1965   *The Red Antway of the Navaho.* Santa Fe: Museum of Navajo Ceremonial Art, Navajo Religion Series 5.

1970   *Blessingway.* Tucson: University of Arizona Press.

1975   *The Mountainway of the Navajo.* Tucson: University of Arizona Press.

Wyman, L., & C. Kluckhohn

1938   *Navaho Classification of Their Song Ceremonials.* Memoirs of American Anthropological Association, no. 50, pp. 1-38.